Severn & Somme
and
War's Embers

Photograph of Gurney dated "Christmas 1917" (GA 5.10.15). Probably that which he refers to in a letter in November 1917 (*WL* 234).

IVOR GURNEY

Severn & Somme

and

War's Embers

edited by R. K. R. Thornton

The Mid Northumberland Arts Group
and Carcanet Press
1997

Severn & Somme and *War's Embers*
were first published in one volume in 1987
this paperback edition published 1997 by
Mid Northumberland Arts Group
Wansbeck Square
Ashington
Northumberland NE63 9XL
in association with
Carcanet Press Ltd
Fourth Floor, Conavon Court
12–16 Blackfriars Street
Manchester M3 5BQ

ISBN 0 904790 92 4 [MidNAG]
ISBN 1 85754 348 3 [Carcanet]
The publishers acknowledge financial assistance
from the Arts Council of England and Northern Arts

Printed and bound in England by
Short Run Press, Exeter

CONTENTS

WAR'S EMBERS

ACKNOWLEDGEMENTS

The editor and publishers would like to thank J. R. Haines, Gurney's literary executor, for his permission to reprint these poems and material from the Gurney Archive; his help goes far beyond that permission in that, like his father, he has fostered an interest in Gurney's work. They would also like to thank the Gloucestershire County Library Service and the staff of the City of Gloucester Public Library, especially Miss Barbara Griffith and Mrs Penny Ely. Thanks are also due to a line of enthusiasts whose work has helped to give Gurney something of the reward and recognition that he longed for but never had in his lifetime. Beginning with Marion Scott, and continuing through Gerald and Joy Finzi, the list must include his past editors, Edmund Blunden and Leonard Clark, his biographer Michael Hurd, the chronicler of his happy relationship with the Chapman family, Anthony Boden, and Liz Ward. Thanks are also due to Hilda Spear and to the Cartography section of Newcastle University Geography Department, especially Mrs O. Teasdale. The editor has special thanks to express to P. J. Kavanagh (and to his wife) not only for his edition of the poems, but also for the work unseen by the public which helps to add some order to that difficult mass of documents which makes up the Gurney Archive. Without that help it would have been a much greater task to add to and correct some of his own information.

The Mid Northumberland Arts Group (MidNAG) is the area arts association for central Northumberland. It is sponsored by Wansbeck District Council, administered by the Leisure and Publicity Department of Wansbeck District Council, and grant-aided by Northern Arts.

A BRIEF CHRONOLOGY

1890   Ivor Bertie Gurney born 28 August at 3 Queen Street, Gloucester, son of a tailor. Alfred Cheesman stood as godfather.

1890s   Move to 19 Barton Street. Attends National School and All Saints Sunday School.

1896   Purchase of family piano.

1899   Graduates to full membership of choir of All Saints.

1900   Wins place in Cathedral Choir, and goes to King's School. Begins to learn organ; meets F. W. Harvey.

1905*ff*   Years of intimacy with Cheesman, and Margaret and Emily Hunt, who encourage his artistic talents.

1906   Articled pupil of Dr Herbert Brewer, organist of Gloucester Cathedral. Herbert Howells a fellow pupil from 1907.

1911   Wins scholarship of £40 per annum to Royal College of Music where he goes in Autumn. Meets Marion Scott.

1912   Friendship with Herbert Howells and Arthur Benjamin. Meets Mrs Voynich. Composes the "Elizas". Early signs of physical and mental illness.

1914   War declared on August 4th. Gurney volunteers but is refused.

1915   Volunteers again and is drafted into the army on February 9th as Private no. 3895 of the 2nd/5th Gloucesters.

        Battalion goes to Northampton in February, Chelmsford in April, Epping in June, and back to Chelmsford in August. Briefly in band in September.

1916	To Tidworth on Salisbury Plain in February and to Park House Camp for Active Service Training. Leaves for France on 25 May. 15 June, first Front line fighting (in the Fauquissart-Laventie sector). In August in hospital for teeth and glasses. Plans book of poems. December to February, has job in Sanitary Section.
1917	April, wounded on Good Friday. Sent to hospital at Rouen for six weeks. Given new number 241281 and transferred to Machine Gun Corps. Battalion moves to Ypres front in August. 10(?) September gassed at St Julien (Passchendaele). Shipped to Bangour War Hospital in Edinburgh. Falls in love with nurse Annie Nelson Drummond. *Severn & Somme* published in November. Transferred to Command Depot at Seaton Delaval.
1918	February, in Newcastle General Hospital for "stomach trouble caused by gas". March, convalescing at Brancepeth Castle. June, in Lord Derby's War Hospital in Warrington. July, transferred to Napsbury War Hospital, St Albans. Discharged in October. Munitions work until Armistice in November.
1919	March, second impression of *Severn & Somme*. May, death of father; publication of *War's Embers*.
	Return to Royal College of Music
1919–22	Variety of temporary jobs: organist, cinema pianist, tax officer, farm labourer. Fluent output of poems and songs. Increasing signs of mental disturbance.
1922	Committed to asylum at Barnwood House in Gloucester in September and transferred to the City of London Mental Hospital at Dartford in Kent. Much writing, some music, many poems and autobiographical-poetical letters of appeal.
1937	Dies at Dartford on 26 December. Buried at Twigworth.

INTRODUCTION

Ivor Gurney published only two books of poems in his lifetime, *Severn & Somme* (1917) and *War's Embers* (1919). Apart from a small number of poems published in periodicals and newspapers, that was the sum of the material upon which his reputation as a poet rested until the first selection of his poetry was made in 1954. His reputation as a musician, and particularly as a writer of song-settings, had fared somewhat better and there was a more substantial body of material and a strong interest in his music. In the last ten years the balance has been adjusting in favour of the poetry, upon which particular attention has been focussed by the publication of P. J. Kavanagh's edition of *Collected Poems of Ivor Gurney* (1982). This gave us a much more wide-ranging view of the types of poetry of which Gurney was capable, and demonstrated the intensity and power as well as the delicacy, poignancy and comedy which make his poetry so lively.

In order to make the point clearly about the size of Gurney's achievement and its quality and range, the later poetry gets pride of place in the *Collected Poems*, but at the cost of not representing as fully as some might like the characteristics of the early books. Only twenty-three of the hundred and four poems which they included were reprinted; and so it seemed worth while to republish on the fiftieth anniversary of Gurney's death complete reprints of these two early volumes which represent his promise and ambition and define his early achievement.

In these volumes Gurney works towards his notion of the matter and manner for poetry, from imitations of Rupert Brooke in "To the Poet Before Battle", through questionings and contradictions of Brooke, to Laforgue-like ironic juxtapositions in poems like "At Reserve Depot". The language and apparently random detail of his poems was criticised in some reviews of the time as too journalistic, but they form the basis of his later style, and counterbalance both his musical gift and his idealistic strain. His attempts to achieve a musical rather than a simply metrical force make the poems always interesting, especially where the conventional lyric and the colloquial in language and rhythm begin to struggle with each other. A good example of this is in his development of what a reviewer called his "diminished double rhyme", which acts rather as Wilfred Owen's half-rhymes do. Gurney probably developed this himself, and it becomes a characteristic feature of his later work, but he may have seen hints of it in the work of others, since he was an assiduous reader of contemporary poetry and responded eagerly to its innovations.

In the letters and appeals which Ivor Gurney wrote from the Asylum where he spent the last fifteen years of his life he repeatedly refers to himself as "War poet", and it is true that much of the poetry which he wrote concerns itself either directly or obliquely with his experiences in France and Belgium in 1916 and 1917. But his poetry is no more limited to war than it is to Gloucester, another of his essential passions which links up with the first in the title and interests of *Severn & Somme*. Comparisons with other poets of the First World War, however, need to recognise the difference between those poems written at the time of the conflict and those poems written afterwards. As Gurney asserted when suggesting that Rupert Brooke would not have developed, "Great poets, great creators are not much influenced by immediate events; those must sink in to the very foundations and be absorbed" (*WL* 34). None the less, Gurney was "hurt into poetry" by his experiences, and to immediate effect. Like many of those who wrote about the war and did not survive it, he wrote of his responses with an urgency which balances the perhaps hasty quality of the technique; but just because he *did* survive the war, we must not forget what he wrote during the war.

At about the time of the publication of *War's Embers*, Gurney reported to Marion Scott that Shanks had told him that Squire considered Gurney the best of the young men just below the horizon (GA 46.30.5). The books here republished indicate the grounds on which that judgement could reasonably be made. They are the poems of a developing poet who is a remarkable musician.

They are also light and lyrical, and it seemed best to keep the poems to the forefront of the book and to leave the notes to the back for those who wish for the wealth of detail that is available on the poems and their publication. The Gurney Archive in Gloucester Public Library is based on the material collected by Marion Scott from her years of correspondence with Gurney and her acting as "Grand Literary Agent" (and also importantly as one who enthusiastically insisted to him that he is both a poet *and* a composer). She collected carefully and so it is possible to follow with some minuteness the process of the poems and the books.

The texts for the poems are taken without alteration from the original editions. Gurney did much later add to, alter, and rewrite some of the poems, but in a way which completely changes the spirit of the books. It seemed best therefore to take the poems as representative of the Gurney of 1917–19. Even without the bias of friendship, what F. W. Harvey wrote of the second book is not too far out: "Though there may be a dozen or so bad lines, there is not a bad poem in the book".

Note The following abbreviations are used throughout the book:

WL Ivor Gurney War Letters, 1983

GA Gurney Archive (Gloucester Public Library)

SEVERN & SOMME

BY

IVOR GURNEY

Private, of the Gloucesters

LONDON : SIDGWICK & JACKSON, LTD.
3 ADAM STREET, ADELPHI, W.C.2.   1917

Facsimile of the title-page from the original edition.

PREFACE

This book stands dedicated to one only of my friends, but there are many others to whom I would willingly dedicate singly and in state, if that did not mean the writing of forty books of verse and dedications—a terrible thing for all concerned.

So that, under the single name and sign of homage and affection, I would desire such readers as come to me to add also:

To my father and mother; F. W. Harvey (also a Gloucestershire lad); Miss Marion Scott, whose criticism has been so useful, and she so kind, in spite of my continued refusal to alter a word of anything; the Vicar of Twigworth; Herbert Howells (and this is not the last time you will hear of him); Mr. Hilaire Belloc, whose "Path to Rome" has been my trench companion, with "The Spirit of Man"; Mr. Wilfred Gibson, author of "Friends," a great little book; many others also, including Shakespeare and Bach, both friends of mine; and, last but not least, my comrades of two platoons of the -/-* Gloucesters, who so often have wondered whether I were crazy or not. Let them draw their own conclusions now, for the writing of this book it was that so distracted me. . . . This is a long list, and even now does not include old Mrs. Poyner, who was so jolly and long-suffering, nor my boat *Dorothy*, now idle in the mud; though a poet sang of her full of glory at Framilode.

Even as I write the list becomes fuller, farther extended, yet a soldier must face pain, and so it remains shorter by far than might be.

I fear that those who buy the book (or even borrow), to get information about the Gloucesters will be disappointed. Most of

* The publication of Battalion Nos. being strictly forbidden by the Military Authorities, we have to leave the identification of the platoons referred to by Mr. Gurney to those whom it concerns.—S. & J., LTD.

the book is concerned with a person named Myself, and the rest with my county, Gloucester, that whether I die or live stays always with me—being in itself so beautiful, so full of memories; whose people are so good to be friends with, so easy-going and so frank.

Some of the afore-mentioned people I have never had good fortune enough to meet in the flesh, but that was not my fault. I hope they will forgive my using their names without permission. Ah, would they only retaliate in kind! That is, however, not likely, as I never was famous, and a Common Private makes but little show.

All these verses were written in France, and in sound of the guns, save only two or three earlier pieces. This should be reason enough to excuse any roughness in the technique. If more reason is required, people of home, and most of all, people of Gloucester, may well be indulgent to one who thought of them so often, and whose images of beauty in the mind were always of Gloucester, county of Cotswold and Severn, and a plain rich, blossomy, and sweet of airs—as the wise Romans knew, who made their homes in exile by the brown river, watching the further bank for signs of war.

IVOR GURNEY
Spring, 1917

To Certain Comrades

(E. S. and J. H.)

Living we loved you, yet withheld our praises
Before your faces;

And though we had your spirits high in honour,
After the English manner

We said no word. Yet, as such comrades would,
You understood.

Such friendship is not touched by Death's disaster,
But stands the faster;

And all the shocks and trials of time cannot
Shake it one jot.

Beside the fire at night some far December,
We shall remember

And tell men, unbegotten as yet, the story
Of your sad glory—

Of your plain strength, your truth of heart, your
     splendid
Coolness, all ended!

All ended, . . . yet the aching hearts of lovers
Joy overcovers,

Glad in their sorrow; hoping that if they must
Come to the dust,

An ending such as yours may be their portion,
And great good fortune—

That if we may not live to serve in peace
England, watching increase—

Then death with you, honoured, and swift, and high;
And so—not die.

In Trenches, July 1916

The Fire Kindled

God, that I might see
   Framilode once again!
Redmarley, all renewed,
   Clear shining after rain.

And Cranham, Cranham trees,
   And blaze of Autumn hues.
Portway under the moon,
   Silvered with freezing dews.

May Hill that Gloster dwellers
   'Gainst every sunset see;
And the wide Severn river
   Homing again to the sea.

The star of afterglow,
   Venus, on western hills;
Dymock in spring: O spring
   Of home! O daffodils!

And Malvern's matchless huge
   Bastions of ancient fires—
These will not let me rest,
   So hot my heart desires. . . .

Here we go sore of shoulder,
    Sore of foot, by quiet streams;
But these are not my rivers. . . .
    And these are useless dreams.

To the Poet before Battle

Now, youth, the hour of thy dread passion comes:
Thy lovely things must all be laid away;
And thou, as others, must face the riven day
Unstirred by rattle of the rolling drums,
Or bugles' strident cry. When mere noise numbs
The sense of being, the fear-sick soul doth sway,
Remember thy great craft's honour, that they may say
Nothing in shame of poets. Then the crumbs
Of praise the little versemen joyed to take
Shall be forgotten: then they must know we are,
For all our skill in words, equal in might
And strong of mettle as those we honoured; make
The name of poet terrible in just war,
And like a crown of honour upon the fight.

Maisemore

O when we swung through Maisemore,
    The Maisemore people cheered,
And women ran from farmyards,
    And men from ricks, afeared

To lose the sight of soldiers
    Who would, 'fore Christmas Day,
Blow Kaiser William's Army
    Like mist of breath away!

The war it was but young then!
    And we were young, unknowing
The path we were to tread,
    The way the path was going.

And not a man of all of us,
    Marching across the bridge,
Had thought how Home would linger
    In our hearts, as Maisemore Ridge.

When the darkness downward hovers
    Making trees like German shadows,
How our souls fly homing, homing
    Times and times to Maisemore meadows,

By Aubers ridge that Maisemore men
    Have died in vain to hold. . . .
The burning thought but once desires
    Maisemore in morning gold!

O when we marched through Maisemore
    Past many a creaking cart,
We little thought we had in us
    Love so hot at heart.

Afterwards

Those dreadful evidences of Man's ill-doing
The kindly Mother of all shall soon hide deep,
Covering with tender fingers her children asleep,
Till Time's slow cycle turns them to renewing
In other forms their beauty—no grief, no rueing
Irrevocable woe. They'll lie, they'll steep
Their hearts in peace unfathomed, till they leap
Quick to the light of the sun, as flowers strewing,

Maybe, their own friends' paths. And that's not all.
When men who knew them walk old ways alone,
The paths they loved together, at even-fall,
The troubled heart shall know a presence near,
Friendly, familiar, and the old grief gone,
The new keen joy shall make all darkness clear.

Carol

Winter now has bared the trees,
    Killed with tiny swords the jolly
Leafage that mid-summer sees,
    But left the ivy and the holly.
        Hold them high
        And make delight
For Christë's joy that's born to-night.

All green things but these have hid
    Their heads, or died in melancholy,
Winter's spite them all has rid
    Save only ivy and brave holly.
        Give them place
        In all men's sight
For Christë's grace that's born to-night.

Baby eyes are pleased to see
    Bright red berries and children jolly,
So shout and dance and sing with glee,
    And honour ivy and prickly holly.
        Honour courage
        And make delight
For Christë's sake that's born to-night.

Christus natus hodie!
Drink deep of joy on Christmas Day,
Join hands and sing a roundelay,
For this is Christ's and children's day.
Christus natus hodie!
Hodie!

Strange Service

Little did I dream, England, that you bore me
Under the Cotswold hills beside the water meadows,
To do you dreadful service, here, beyond your borders
And your enfolding seas.

I was a dreamer ever, and bound to your dear service,
Meditating deep, I thought on your secret beauty,
As through a child's face one may see the clear spirit
Miraculously shining.

Your hills not only hills, but friends of mine and kindly,
Your tiny knolls and orchards hidden beside the river
Muddy and strongly-flowing, with shy and tiny
        streamlets
Safe in its bosom.

Now these are memories only, and your skies and rushy
        sky-pools
Fragile mirrors easily broken by moving airs. . . .
In my deep heart for ever goes on your daily being,
And uses consecrate.

Think on me too, O Mother, who wrest my soul to serve
    you
In strange and fearful ways beyond your encircling
    waters;
None but you can know my heart, its tears and sacrifice;
None, but you, repay.

Serenity

Nor steel nor flame has any power on me,
Save that its malice work the Almighty Will,
Nor steel nor flame has any power on me;
Through tempests of hell-fire I must go free
And unafraid; so I remember still
Nor steel nor flame has any power on me,
Save that its malice work the Almighty Will.

The Signaller's Vision

One rainy winter dusk
    Mending a parted cable,
Sudden I saw so clear
    Home and the tea-table.

So clear it was, so sweet,
    I did not start, but drew
The breath of deep content
    Some minutes ere I knew

My Mother's face that's soother
    Than autumn half-lights kind,
My softly smiling sisters
    Who keep me still in mind,

Were but a dream, a vision—
That faded.   And I knew
The smell of trench, trench-feeling—
And turned to work anew.

The Mother

We scar the earth with dreadful engin'ry;
She takes us to her bosom at the last;
Hiding our hate with love, who cannot see
Of any child the faults; and holds us fast.
We'll wait in quiet till our passion's past.

To England—a Note

I watched the boys of England where they went
Through mud and water to do appointed things.
See one a stake, and one wire-netting brings,
And one comes slowly under a burden bent
Of ammunition. Though the strength be spent
They "carry on" under the shadowing wings
Of Death the ever-present. And hark, one sings
Although no joy from the grey skies be lent.

Are these the heroes—these? have kept from you
The power of primal savagery so long?
Shall break the devil's legions? These they are
Who do in silence what they might boast to do;
In the height of battle tell the world in song
How they do hate and fear the face of War.

Bach and the Sentry

Watching the dark my spirit rose in flood
  On that most dearest Prelude of my delight.
The low-lying mist lifted its hood,
  The October stars showed nobly in clear night.

When I return, and to real music-making,
  And play that Prelude, how will it happen then?
Shall I feel as I felt, a sentry hardly waking,
  With a dull sense of No Man's Land again?

Letters

"Mail's up!" The vast of night is over,
And love of friends fills all one's mind.
(His wife, his sister, or his lover.)
Mail's up, the vast of night is over,
The grey-faced heaven joy does cover
With love, and God once more seems kind.
"Mail's up!" the vast of night is over,
And love of friends fills all one's mind.

Strafe

The "crumps" are falling twenty to the minute.
We crouch, and wait the end of it—or us.
Just behind the trench, before, and in it,
The "crumps" are falling twenty to the minute;
(O Framilode! O Maisemore's laughing linnet!)
Here comes a monster like a motor-bus.
The "crumps" are falling twenty to the minute:
We crouch and wait the end of it—or us.

Acquiescence

Since I can neither alter my destiny
By one hair's breadth from its appointed course;
Since bribes nor prayers nor any earthly force
May from its pathway move a life not free—
I must gather together the whole strength of me,
My senses make my willing servitors;
Cherish and feed the better, starve the worse;
Turn all my pride to proud humility.
Meeting the daily shocks and frozen, stony,
Cynical face of doubt with smiles and joy—
As a battle with autumn winds delights a boy,
Before the smut of the world and the lust of money,
Power, and fame, can yet his youth destroy;
Ere he has scorned his Father's patrimony.

The Strong Thing

I have seen Death and the faces of men in fear
    Of Death, and shattered, terribly ruined flesh,
Appalled; but through the horror, coloured and clear
    The love of my county, Gloster, rises afresh.

And on the Day of Days, the Judgment Day,
    The Word of Doom awaiting breathless and still,
I'll marvel how sweet's the air down Framilode way,
    And take my sentence on sheer-down Crickley Hill.

Scots

The boys who laughed and jested with me but yesterday,
So fit for kings to speak to, so blithe and proud and
        gay. . . .
Are now but thoughts of blind pain, and best hid
        away. . . .
(Over the top this morning at the dawn's first grey.)

O, if we catch the Kaiser his dirty hide to flay,
We'll hang him on a tall tree his pride to allay.
That will not bring the boys again to mountain and
        brae. . . .
(Over the top this morning at the dawn's first grey.)

To think—earth's best and dearest turned to red broken
        clay
By one devil's second! What words can we say?
Or what gift has God their mothers' anguish to
        repay? . . .
(Over the top this morning at the first flush of day.)

To an Unknown Lady

You that were once so sweet, are sweeter now
That an even leaden greyness clouds my days;
A pain it is to think on your sweet ways,
Your careless-tender speaking, tender and low.
When the hills enclosed us, hid in happy valleys,
Greeting a thousand times the things most dear,
We wasted thoughts of love in laughter clear,
And told our passion out in mirthful sallies.
But in me now a burning impulse rages
To praise our love in words like flaming gold,

Molten and live for ever; not fit for cold
And coward like-to-passions Time assuages.
Nor do I fear you are lovely only in dreams,
Being as the sky reflected in clear streams.

Song and Pain

Out of my sorrow have I made these songs,
    Out of my sorrow;
Though somewhat of the making's eager pain
    From Joy did borrow.

Some day, I trust, God's purpose of Pain for me
    Shall be complete,
And then—to enter in the House of Joy. . . .
    Prepare, my feet.

Purple and Black

The death of princes is
    Honoured most greatly,
Proud kings put purple on
    In manner stately.

Though they have lived such life
    As God offends,
Gone fearful down to death,
    Sick, without friends.

And in the temple dim,
    Trumpets of gold
Proclaim their glory; so
    Their story is told.

In sentimental hymns
    Weeping her dolour,
The mother of heroes wears
    Vile black—Death's colour,

Who should walk proudly with
    The noblest one
Of all that purple throng—
    "This was my son."

West Country

Spring comes soon to Maisemore
    And spring comes sweet,
With bird-songs and blue skies,
    On gay dancing feet;
But she is such a shy lady
    I fear we'll never meet.

Yet some day round a corner
    Where the hedge foams white,
I'll find Spring sleeping
    In the young-crescent night,
And seize her and make her
    Yield all her delight.

But yon's a glad story
    That's yet to be told.
Here's grey winter's bareness
    And no-shadowed cold.
O Spring, with your music,
    Your blue, green, and gold,
Come shame his hard wisdom
    With laughter and gold!

Firelight

Silent, bathed in firelight, in dusky light and gloom
The boys squeeze together in the smoky dirty room,
Crowded round the fireplace, a thing of bricks and tin,
They watch the shifting embers till the good dreams
      enter in,

That fill the low hovel with blossoms fresh with dew,
And blue sky and white clouds that sail the clear air
      through.
They talk of daffodillies and the bluebells' skiey bed,
Till silence thrills and murmurs at the things they have
      said.

And yet, they have no skill of words, whose eyes glow so
      deep,
They wait for night and silence and the strange power of
      sleep,
To lift them and drift them like sea-birds over the sea
Where some day I shall walk again, and they walk with
      me.

The Estaminet

The crowd of us were drinking
    One night at Riez Bailleul,
The glasses were a-clinking,
    The estaminet was full;

And loud with song and story
    And blue with tales and smoke,—
We spoke no word of glory,
    Nor mentioned "foreign yoke."

But yarns of girls in Blighty;
    Vain, jolly, ugly, fair,
Standoffish, foolish, flighty—
    And O! that we were there!

Where never thuds a "Minnie,"
    But Minnie smiles at you
A-meeting in the spinney,
    With kisses not a few.

And of an inn that Johnson
    Does keep; the "Rising Sun."
His friends him call Jack Johnson,
    He's Gloster's only one.

And talk of poachers' habits
    (But girls ever and again)
Of killing weasels, rabbits,
    Stoats, pheasants, never men,

Although we knew to-morrow
    Must take us to the line,
In beer hid thought and sorrow,
    In ruddy and white wine.

When all had finished drinking,
    Though still was clear each head,
We said no word—went slinking
    Straight homeward (?), into bed (?).

O never lads were merrier,
    Nor straighter nor more fine,
Though we were only "Terrier"
    And only, "Second Line."

O I may get to Blighty,
    Or hell, without a sign
Of all the love that filled me,
    Leave dumb the love that filled me,
The flood of love that filled me
    For these dear comrades of mine.

Song

Only the wanderer
    Knows England's graces,
Or can anew see clear
    Familiar faces.

And who loves joy as he
    That dwells in shadows?
Do not forget me quite,
    O Severn meadows.

Ballad of the Three Spectres

As I went up by Ovillers
    In mud and water cold to the knee,
There went three jeering, fleering spectres,
    That walked abreast and talked of me.

The first said, "Here's a right brave soldier
    That walks the dark unfearingly;
Soon he'll come back on a fine stretcher,
    And laughing for a nice Blighty."

The second, "Read his face, old comrade,
    No kind of lucky chance I see;

One day he'll freeze in mud to the marrow,
    Then look his last on Picardie."

Though bitter the word of these first twain
    Curses the third spat venomously;
"He'll stay untouched till the war's last dawning
    Then live one hour of agony."

Liars the first two were. Behold me
    At sloping arms by one—two—three;
Waiting the time I shall discover
    Whether the third spake verity.

Communion

Beauty lies so deep
    On all the fields,
Nothing for the eyes
    But blessing yields.

Tall elms, greedy of light,
    Stand tip-toe. See
The last light linger in
    Their tracery.

The guns are dumb, are still
    All evil noises.
The singing heart in peace
    Softly rejoices,

Only unsatisfied
    With Beauty's hunger
And sacramental thirst—
    Nothing of anger.

Mist wraiths haunt the path
 As daylight lessens,
The stars grow clearer, and
 My dead friend's presence.

Time and the Soldier

How slow you move, old Time;
 Walk a bit faster!
Old fool, I'm not your slave. . . .
 Beauty's my master!

You hold me for a space. . . .
 What are you, Time?
A ghost, a thing of thought,
 An easy rhyme.

Some day I shall again,
 For all your scheming,
See Severn valley clouds
 Like banners streaming.

And walk in Cranham lanes,
 By Maisemore go. . . .
But, fool, decrepit Fool,
 You are so SLOW!!!

Influences

When woods of home grow dark,
 I grow dark too.
Images of strange power
Fill me and thrill me that hour,
 Sombre of hue.

The woods of Dunsinane
   I walk, and know
What storms did shake Macbeth,
That brought on Duncan's death,
   And his own woe.

Strange whispers chill the blood
   Of evil breath;
Such rumours as did stir
Witch and foul sorcerer
   On the lone heath.

No power have these on me;
   I know too well
Their weakness to condemn.
Spring will exorcise them
   With one bluebell.

After-glow
(To F. W. Harvey)

Out of the smoke and dust of the little room
With tea-talk loud and laughter of happy boys,
I passed into the dusk. Suddenly the noise
Ceased with a shock, left me alone in the gloom,
To wonder at the miracle hanging high
Tangled in twigs, the silver crescent clear.—
Time passed from mind. Time died; and then we were
Once more at home together, you and I.

The elms with arms of love wrapped us in shade
Who watched the ecstatic West with one desire,
One soul uprapt; and still another fire
Consumed us, and our joy yet greater made:
That Bach should sing for us, mix us in one
The joy of firelight and the sunken sun.

Hail and Farewell

The destined bullet wounded him,
    They brought him down to die,
Far-off a bugle sounded him
    "Retreat," Good-bye.

Strange, that from ways so hated,
    And tyranny so hard
Should come this strangely fated
    And farewell word.

He thought, "Some Old Sweat might
    Have thrilled at heart to hear,
Gone down into the night
    Too proud to fear!

But I—the fool at arms,
    Musician, poet to boot,
Who hail release; what charms
    In this salute?"

He smiled—"The latest jest
    That time on me shall play."
And watched the dying west,
    Went out with the day.

Praise

O friends of mine, if men mock at my name,
Say "Children loved him."
Since by that word you will have far removed him
From any bitter shame.

Winter Beauty

I cannot live with Beauty out of mind;
    I seek her and desire her all the day,
Being the chiefest treasure man may find,
    And word most sweet his eager lips can say.
She is as strong on me as though I wandered
    In Severn meadows some blue riotous day.

But since the trees have long since lost their green,
    And I, an exile, can but dream of things
Grown magic in the mind, I watch the sheen
    Of frost and hear the song Orion sings,
And hear the star-born passion of Beethoven;
    Man's consolations sung on the quivering strings.

Beauty of song remembered, sunset glories,
    Mix in my mind, till I not care nor know
Whether the stars do move me, golden stories,
    Or ruddy Cotswold in the sunset glow.
I am uprapt, and not my own, immortal, . . .
    In winds of Beauty swinging to and fro.

Beauty immortal, not to be hid, desire
    Of all men, each in his fashion, give me the strong
Thirst past satisfaction for thee, and fire
    Not to be quenched. . . . O lift me, bear me along,
Touch me, make me worthy that men may seek me
    For Beauty, Mistress Immortal, Healer of Wrong.

Song of Pain and Beauty

(To M. M. S.)

O may these days of pain,
　These wasted-seeming days,
Somewhere reflower again
　With scent and savour of praise.
Draw out of memory all bitterness
　Of night with Thy sun's rays.

And strengthen Thou in me
　The love of men here found,
And eager charity,
　That, out of difficult ground,
Spring like flowers in barren deserts, or
　Like light, or a lovely sound.

A simpler heart than mine
　Might have seen beauty clear
Where I could see no sign
　Of Thee, but only fear.
Strengthen me, make me to see Thy beauty always
　In every happening here.

In Trenches, March 1917

Spring. Rouen, May 1917

I am dumb, I am dumb!
And here's a Norman orchard and here's Spring
Goading the sullen words that will not come.
Romance, beating his distant magical drum,
Calls to a soldier bearing alien arms,
"Throw off your yoke and hear my darlings sing,
Blackbirds" (by red-roofed farms)

"More drunk than any poet with May's delight,
Green alive to the eye, and pink and white."

  Joy's there, but not for me;
And song, but shall I sing
That live as in a dream of some bad night,
Whose memories are of such ecstasy
And height of passionate joy, that pain alone
Is born of beauty in cloud and flower and tree;
Yes, and the great Cathedral's towering stone.

To me these are but shadows
Of orchards and old meadows
Trodden before the dawn,
Trodden after the dusk. . . .
All loveliness of France is as a husk,
The inner living spirit of beauty gone,
To that familiar beauty now withdrawn
From exiles hungering ever for the sight
Of her day-face;
England's;
Or in some orchard space
Breathless to drink peace from her calm night.

How shall I sing, since she sings not to me
Songs any more?
High rule she holds for ever on the sea
That's hers, but dreams too might guard the shore
Of France, that's French and set apart for ever.
A Spirit of Love our link of song does sever.
Had it been hate
(The weakest of all sworn enemies of Love)
We should have broken through or passed above
Its foolish barriers;
Here we must bow as to established Fate,
And reverently; for, comrades and high peers,
Sisters in blood,

Our mothers brook no rival in their state
Of motherhood.

But not for ever shall our travail last,
And not for ever we
Be held by iron Duty over sea.
The image of evil shall be overcast,
And all his willing slaves and priests of evil
Scattered like dust, shall lie upon the plain;
That image, ground to dust utterly level
With unregarded weeds and all as vain.

The oppressed shall lift their hearts up once again,
And we return. . . .
Not to scarred lands and homes laid in the dust,
Not with hard hearts to sights that sear and burn,
But with assured longing and certain trust,
To England's royal grace and dignity,
To England's changing skies, rich greenery,
High strength controlled, queenly serenity,
Inviolate kept by her confederate sea
And hearts resolved to every sacrifice.
We shall come home,
We shall come home again,
Living and dead, one huge victorious host—
The dead that would not leave their comrades till
The last steep were topped of the difficult hill,
The last farthing paid of the Great Cost,
The last thrill suffered of the Great Pain.
Living and dead, we shall come home at last
To her sweet breast,
England's; by one touch be paid in full
For all things grey and long and terrible
Of that dread night which seemed eternity.

O Mother, shall thy kisses not restore
Body and life-sick soul? Yes, and set free

Songs and great floods of lovelier melody
Than thou didst give
When we those days of half-awake did live.
And joy must surely flower again more fair
To us, who dwelt in shadows and foul air.
We'll breathe and drink in song.

Spring shall blot out all traces of old care;
Her clouds of green and waves of gold among
We shall grow free of heart, and great, and young—
Be made anew in that Great Resurrection,
Perfect as is the violet's perfection.
Perfect as she
Who sanctifies our memory with sorrow,
Hugs, as a mother hugs, the thoughts that harrow,
Watching for dawn, hungering for the morrow
Lone oversea. . . .

I am dumb now, dumb,
But in that time what music shall not come?
Mother of Beauty, Mistress of the Sea.

June - To - Come

When the sun's fire and gold
    Sets the bee humming,
I will not write to tell
    Him that I'm coming,

But ride out unawares
    On that old road,
Of Minsterworth, of Peace,
    Of Framilode,

And walk, not looked for, in
   That cool, dark passage.
Never a single word;
   Myself my message.

And then; well . . . O we'll drift
   And stand and gaze,
And wonder how we could
   In those Bad Days

Live without Minsterworth;
   Or western air
Fanning the hot cheek,
   Stirring the hair;

In land where hate of men
   God's love did cover;
This land. . . . And here's my dream
   Irrevocably over.

"Hark, Hark, the Lark"

Hark, hark, the lark to heaven's gate uprisen,
   Pours out his joy . . .
I think of you, shut in some distant prison,
   O Boy, poor Boy;

Your heart grown sick with hope deferred and shadows
   Of prison ways;
Not daring to snatch a thought of Severn meadows,
   Or old blue-days.

Song at Morning

Praise for the day's magnificent uprising!
Praise for the cool
Air and the blue new-old ever-surprising
Face of the sky, and mirrored blue of the pool.
Only the fool, bat-witted, owl-eyed fool
Can hold a deaf ear while life begins
The actual opening of a myriad stories. . . .
Blindness, ingratitude, the foolishest sins!
Now if this day blot out my chief desires,
And leave me maimed and blind and full of hot
Surges of insurrection, evil fires,
Memories of joys that seem better forgot;
Quiet me then.
Thy Will is binding on the nearest flower
As on the farthest star; and what shall put me
Out of Thy power, or from Thy guidance far,
Though I in hell of my self-will would shut me?
But if Thy Will be joy for me to-day,
Give me clear eyes, a heart open to feel
Thy influence, Thy kindess: O unseal
The shut, the hidden places in me, reveal
Those things most precious secretly hidden away
From all save children and the simply wise.
Give me clear eyes!
And strength to know, whatever may befall,
The eternal presence of great mysteries,
Glorifying Thee for all.

Trees

("You cannot think how ghastly these battle-fields look under a grey sky. Torn trees are the most terrible things I have ever seen. Absolute blight and curse is on the face of everything.")

The dead land oppressed me;
    I turned my thoughts away,
And went where hill and meadow
    Are shadowless and gay.

Where Coopers stands by Cranham,
    Where the hill-gashes white
Show golden in the sunshine,
    Our sunshine—God's delight.

Beauty my feet stayed at last
    Where green was most cool,
Trees worthy of all worship
    I worshipped . . . then, O fool,

Let my thoughts slide unwitting
    To other, dreadful trees, . . .
And found me standing, staring
    Sick of heart—at these!

Requiem

Pour out your light, O stars, and do not hold
    Your loveliest shining from earth's outworn shell—
Pure and cold your radiance, pure and cold
    My dead friend's face as well.

Requiem

Nor grief nor tears should wrong the silent dead
   Save England's, for her children fallen so far
From her eager care; though by God's justice led
   And fallen in such a war.

Requiem

Pour out your bounty, moon of radiant shining
   On all this shattered flesh, these quiet forms;
For these were slain, so strangely still reclining,
   In the noblest cause was ever waged with arms.

Sonnets 1917

(To the Memory of Rupert Brooke)

1. FOR ENGLAND

Though heaven be packed with joy-bewildering
Pleasures of soul and heart and mind, yet who
Would willingly let slip, freely let go
Earth's mortal loveliness; go wandering
Where never the late bird is heard to sing,
Nor full-sailed cloud-galleons wander slow;
No pathways in the woods; no afterglow,
When the air's fire and magic with sense of spring?

So the dark horror clouds us, and the dread
Of the unknown. . . . But if it must be, then
What better passing than to go out like men
For England, giving all in one white glow?
Whose bodies shall lie in earth as on a bed,
And as the Will directs our spirits may go.

2. PAIN

Pain, pain continual; pain unending;
Hard even to the roughest, but to those
Hungry for beauty. . . . Not the wisest knows,
Nor most pitiful-hearted, what the wending
Of one hour's way meant. Grey monotony lending
Weight to the grey skies, grey mud where goes
An army of grey bedrenched scarecrows in rows
Careless at last of cruellest Fate-sending.
Seeing the pitiful eyes of men foredone,
Or horses shot, too tired merely to stir,
Dying in shell-holes both, slain by the mud.
Men broken, shrieking even to hear a gun.—
Till pain grinds down, or lethargy numbs her,
The amazed heart cries angrily out on God.

3. SERVITUDE

If it were not for England, who would bear
This heavy servitude one moment more?
To keep a brothel, sweep and wash the floor
Of filthiest hovels were noble to compare
With this brass-cleaning life. Now here, now there
Harried in foolishness, scanned curiously o'er
By fools made brazen by conceit, and store
Of antique witticisms thin and bare.

Only the love of comrades sweetens all,
Whose laughing spirit will not be outdone.
As night-watching men wait for the sun
To hearten them, so wait I on such boys
As neither brass nor Hell-fire may appal,
Nor guns, nor sergeant-major's bluster and noise.

4. HOME-SICKNESS

When we go wandering the wide air's blue spaces,
Bare, unhappy, exiled souls of men;
How will our thoughts over and over again
Return to Earth's familiar lovely places,
Where light with shadow ever interlaces—
No blanks of blue, nor ways beyond man's ken—
Where birds are, and flowers, as violet, and wren,
Blackbird, bluebell, hedge-sparrow, tiny daisies.

O tiny things, but very stuff of soul
To us . . . so frail. . . . Remember what we are;
Set us not on some strange outlandish star,
But one caring for Love. Give us a Home.
There we may wait while the long ages roll
Content, unfrightened by vast Time-to-come.

5. ENGLAND THE MOTHER

We have done our utmost, England, terrible
And dear taskmistress, darling Mother and stern.
The unnoticed nations praise us, but we turn
Firstly, only to thee—"Have we done well?
Say, are you pleased?"—and watch your eyes that tell
To us all secrets, eyes sea-deep that burn
With love so long denied; with tears discern
The scars and haggard look of all that hell.

Thy love, thy love shall cherish, make us whole,
Whereto the power of Death's destruction is weak.
Death impotent, by boys bemocked at, who
Will leave unblotted in the soldier-soul
Gold of the daffodil, the sunset streak,
The innocence and joy of England's blue.

WAR'S EMBERS

AND OTHER VERSES

BY

IVOR GURNEY

London : SIDGWICK & JACKSON, LTD.

3 ADAM STREET, ADELPHI, W.C.2.   1919

Facsimile of the title-page from the original edition.

To M. M. S.

O, if my wishes were my power,
You should be praised as were most fit,
Whose kindness cannot help but flower.

But since the fates have ordered it
Otherwise, then ere the hour
Of darkness deaden all my wit

I'll write: how all my art was poor,
My mind too thought-packed to acquit
My debt . . . And only, "Thanks once more."

The Volunteer

(To A. L. B.)

I would test God's purposes:
    I will go up and see
What fate He'll give, what destiny
    His hand holds for me.

For God is very secret,
    Slow-smiles, but does not say
A word that will foreshadow
    Shape of the coming day.

Curious am I, curious . . .
    And since He will not tell
I'll prove Him, go up against
    The naked mouth of Hell.

And what hereafter—Heaven?
    Or Blighty? O if it were . . .
Mere agony, mere pain the price
    Of the returning there.

Or—nothing! Days in mud
    And slush, then other days . . .
Aie me! "Are they not all
    The seas of God"; God's Ways?

The Farm

(To Mrs Harvey and Those Others)

A creeper-covered house, an orchard near;
A farmyard with tall ricks upstanding clear
In golden sunlight of a late September.—

How little of a whole world to remember!
How slight a thing to keep a spirit free!
Within the house were books,
A piano, dear to me,
And round the house the rooks
Haunted each tall elm tree;
Each sunset crying, calling, clamouring aloud.

And friends lived there of whom the house was proud,
Sheltering with content from wind and storm,
Them loving gathered at the hearthside warm,
(O friendly, happy crowd!)
Caress of firelight gave them, touching hair
And cheeks and hands with sombre gleams of love.
(When day died out behind the lovely bare
Network of twigs, orchard and elms apart;
When rooks lay still in round dark nests above,
And Peace like cool dew comforted the heart.)

The house all strangers welcomed, but as strangers kept
For ever them apart
From its deep heart,
That hidden sanctuary of love close guarded;
Having too great a honey-heap uphoarded
Of children's play, men's work, lightly to let
Strangers therein;
Who knew its stubborn pride, and loved the more
The place from webbed slate roof to cellar floor—
Hens clucking, ducks, all casual farmyard din.
How empty the place seemed when Duty called
To harder service its three sons than tending
Brown fruitful good earth there! But all's God's sending.
Above the low barn where the oxen were stalled
The old house watched for weeks the road, to see
Nothing but common traffic; nothing its own.
It had grown to them so used, so long had known
Their presences; sheltered and shared sorrow and glee,

No wonder it felt desolate and left alone . . .
That must remember, nothing at all forget.
My mind (how often!) turned and returned to it,
When in queer holes of chance, bedraggled, wet,
Lousy I lay; to think how by Severn-side
A house of steadfastness and quiet pride
Kept faith to friends (when hope of mine had died
Almost to ash). And never twilight came
With mystery and peace and points of flame—
Save it must bring sounds of my Severn flowing
Steadily seawards, orange windows glowing
Bright in the dusk, and many a well-known name.

Omens

(To E. H.)

Black rooks about the trees
    Are circling slow;
Tall elms that can no ease
    Nor comfort know,
Since that the Autumn wind
Batters them before, behind,
A bitter breeze unkind.

They call like tongues of dread
    Prophesying woe,
Rooks on the sunset red,
    Not heeding how
Their clamouring brings near
To a woman the old fear
For her far soldier dear.

That harsh and idle crying
    Of mere annoy

Tells her how men are dying,
    And how her boy
May lie, his racked thought turning
To the home fire on the hearth burning,
The last agony be learning.

Eternal Treasure

(To H. N. H.)

Why think on Beauty as for ever lost
When fire and steel have worked their evil will,
Since Beauty lasts beyond decaying dust,
And in the after-dark is lovely still?
We are no phantoms; Body is but the case
Of an immortal Flame that does not perish,
Can the all-withering power of Time outface,
Since God Himself with love that flame does cherish.
Take comfort then, and dare the dangerous thing,
Death flouting with his impotence of wrath;
For Beauty arms us 'gainst his envious sting,
Safes us in any the most perilous path.
Come then, O brothers, greet what may befall
With Joy, for Beauty's Maker ordereth all.

Fire in the Dusk

When your white hands have lost their fairy power,
Like dimpling water flash and charm no more,
Quick pride of grace is still, closed your bright eyes—
I still must think, under those Northern skies,
Some influence shall remain of all that sweet;
Some flower of courage braving Easter sleet;

Colour to stir tears in tenderest skies;
Music of light. Your Autumn beeches shall
Set passion blazing in a heart until
Colour you gave be fashioned in formal line
On line; another's beauty prove divine,
And all your wandering grace shall not be lost
To earth, being too precious, too great of cost—
Last wonder to awake the divine spark,
A lovely presence lighting Summer's dark;
Though dust your frame of flesh, such dust as makes
Blue radiance of March in hidden brakes. . . .
Pass from your body then, be what you will,
Whose light-foot walk outdanced the daffodil,
Since Time can but confirm you and fulfil
That hidden crescent power in you—Old Time,
Spoiler of pride, and towers, and breath, and rhyme,
Yet on the spirit impotent of power and will.

Turmut-hoeing

I straightened my back from turmut-hoeing
    And saw, with suddenly opened eyes,
Tall trees, a meadow ripe for mowing,
    And azure June's cloud-circled skies.

Below, the earth was beautiful
    Of touch and colour, fair each weed,
But Heaven's high beauty held me still,
    Only of music had I need.

And the white-clad girl at the old farm,
    Who smiled and looked across at me,
Dumb was held by that strong charm
    Of cloud-ships sailing a foamless sea.

In a Ward

(To J. W. H.)

O wind that tosses free
  The children's hair;
Scatters the blossom of
  Apple and pear;
Blow in my heart, touch me,
  Gladden me here.

You have seen so many things—
  Blow in and tell
Tales of white sand and golden
  'Gainst the sea swell.
Bring me fine meadow-thoughts,
  Fresh orchard smell.

Here we must stare through glass
  To see the sun—
Stare at flat ceilings white
  Till day is done:
While you, sunshine, starshine,
  May out and run.

Blow in and bring us all
  Dear home-delight—
Green face of the Spring earth,
  Blue of deep night.
Blot each of our faces
  From the others' sight.

Camps

Out of the line we rest in villages
    Quiet indeed, where heal the spirit's scars;
But even so, lapped deep in sunshine and ease,
    We are haunted for ever by the shapes of wars.

Green in the sun they lie, secret, deserted,
    Lovely against the blue the summits show,
Where once the bright steel sang, the red blood spurted,
    And brave men cowed their terrors long ago.

By day their life was easy; but at night,
    Even now, one hears strange rustlings in the bush;
And, straining tensely doubtful ear and sight,
    The stealthy moving ere the sudden rush;

And flinches from the spear. War's just-bright embers
    That Earth still keeps and treasures for the pride
In sacrifice there shown; with love remembers
    The beauty and quick strength of men that died.

Who died as we may die, for Freedom, beauty
    Of common living, calmly led in peace,
Yet took the flinty road and hard of duty,
    Whose end was life abundant and increase.

But—when Heaven's gate wide opening receives us
    Victors and full of song, forgetting scars;
Shall we see to stir old memories, to grieve us,
    Heaven's never-yet-healed sores of Michael's wars?

Girl's Song

The tossing poplar in the wind
    Shows underleaf of silver-white;
The roughness of the wind unkind
    Torments her out of all delight.
But O that he were here
Whose blows and whose caresses alike were dear!

The great oak to the tearing blast
    Stands steady with strong arms held wide,
So over him my anger passed,
    When his rough usage hurt my pride.
But O that once again
I might arouse that passion, endure that pain!

Solace of Men

Sweet smelling, sweet to handle, fair of hue
    Tobacco is. The soldier everywhere
    Takes it as friend, its friendliness to share,
Whether in fragrant wreaths it mount faint blue
In dug-out low, or surreptitiously to
    Parapet in rimy night, from hidden lair
    Of sentry; staying hunger, stilling fear—
The old dreams of comfort bringing anew.
For from that incense grows the stuff of dreams,
    And in those clouds a drowsing man may find
    All that was ever sweet to his starved mind,
        Heart long denied—dear friends, hills, horses, trees,
Slopes of brown ploughland, sunset's fading gleams . . .
        The bane of care, the spur to memories.

Day-boys and Choristers

(To the Boys of King's School, Gloucester, 1900–1905)

Under the shade of the great Tower
    Where pass the goodly and the wise,
Year in, year out, winter and summer,
    With scufflings and excited cries,
Football rages, not told in pages
    Of Fame whereof the wide world hears;
A battle of divided Empire—
    The day-boys and the choristers.

CHORUS
So here's to the room where the dark beams cross over,
    And here's to the cupboard where hides the cane;
The paddock and fives-court, great chestnut, tall tower—
    When Fritz stops his fooling we'll see them again.

Golf balls, tennis balls, cricket and footballs,
    Balls of all sizes and sorts were sent
Soaring by wall and arch and ivy
    High, high over to banishment.
(Poor owner that loses!) And oh! but the bruises,
    Scars, and red hacks to cover the brave
Shins of the boldest, when up and down playground
    Victory surged, Victory, edged like a wave.

CHORUS
So here's to the room where the dark beams cross over,
    And here's to the cupboard where hides the cane,
The paddock and fives-court, great chestnut, tall tower—
    When Fritz stops his fooling we'll see them again.

Little they knew, those boys, how in Flanders
    And plains of France, in another day
A trial dreadful of nerve and sinew

For four long years should test alway
That playtime pluck, that yet should carry
    Them through Hell's during worst, and how
Europe should honour them, a whole world praise them,
    Though Death tore their bodies and laid them low.

CHORUS
So here's to the room where the dark beams cross over,
    And here's to the cupboard where hides the cane;
The paddock and fives-court, great chestnut, tall tower—
    When Fritz stops his fooling we'll see them again.

At Reserve Depot

When Spring comes here with early innocency
    Of pale high blue, they'll put Revally back.
The passers-by carelessly amused will see
    Breakfastless boys killing the patient sack.

And there will be manœuvres where the violet shows,
    Hiding its dark fervour, guarding its flame,
Where I shall lie and stare while the mystery grows
    Huge and more huge, till the Sergeant calls my name.

Toasts and Memories

(To the Men of the 2/5 Gloucester Regiment)

When once I sat in estaminets
    With trusty friends of mine,
We drank to folk in England
    And pledged them well in wine,

While thoughts of Gloucester filled us—
    Roads against windy skies
At sunset, Severn river,
    Red inn-blinds, country cries.

That stung the heart with sorrow
    And barbéd sweet delight
At Riez Bailleul, Laventie,
    At Merville, many a night.

Now I am over Channel
    I cannot help but think
Of friends who stifle longing
    With friendly food and drink.

"Where's Gurney now, I wonder,
    That smoked a pipe all day;
Sometimes that talked like blazes,
    Sometimes had naught to say?"

And I, at home, must wonder
    Where all my comrades are:
Those men whose Heart-of-Beauty
    Was never stained by War.

From the Window

Tall poplars in the sun
Are quivering, and planes,
Forgetting the day gone,
Its cold un-August rains;
But with me still remains
The sight of beaten corn,
Crushed flowers and forlorn,
The summer's wasted gains—

Yet pools in secret lanes
Abrim with heavenly blue
Life's wonder mirror anew.
I must forget the pains
Of yesterday, and do
Brave things—bring loaded wains
The bare brown meadows through,
I must haste, I must out and run,
Wonder, till my heart drains
Joy's cup, as in high champagnes
Of blue, where great clouds go on
With white sails free from stains
Full-stretched, on fleckless mains—
With captain's joy of some proud galleon.

Ypres–Minsterworth

(To F. W. H.)

Thick lie in Gloucester orchards now
    Apples the Severn wind
With rough play tore from the tossing
    Branches, and left behind
Leaves strewn on pastures, blown in hedges,
    And by the roadway lined.

And I lie leagues on leagues afar
    To think how that wind made
Great shoutings in the wide chimney,
    A noise of cannonade—
Of how the proud elms by the signpost
    The tempest's will obeyed—

To think how in some German prison
   A boy lies with whom
I might have taken joy full-hearted
   Hearing the great boom
Of Autumn, watching the fire, talking
   Of books in the half gloom.

O wind of Ypres and of Severn
   Riot there also, and tell
Of comrades safe returned, home-keeping
   Music and Autumn smell.
Comfort blow him and friendly greeting,
   Hearten him, wish him well!

Near Midsummer

Severn's most fair to-day!
See what a tide of blue
She pours, and flecked alway
With gold, and what a crew
Of seagulls snowy white
Float round her to delight
Villagers, travellers.
A brown thick flood is hers
In winter when the rains
Wash down from Midland plains,
Halting wayfarers,
Low meadows flooding deep
With torrents from the steep
Mountains of Wales and small
Hillocks of no degree—
Streams jostling to the sea;
(Wrangling yet brotherly).
Blue June has altered all—
The river makes its fall

With murmurous still sound,
Past Pridings faëry ground,
And steep-down Newnham cliff. . . .
O Boys in trenches, if
You could see what any may
(Escaping town for the day),
Strong Severn all aglow,
But tideless, running slow:
Far Cotswolds all a-shimmer,
Blue Bredon leagues away—
Huge Malverns, farther, dimmer. . . .
Then you would feel the fire
Of the First Days inspire
You, when, despising all
Save England's, honour's call,
You dared the worst for her:
Faced all things without fear,
So she might stand alway
A free Mother of men;
High Queen as on this day.
There would flood through you again
The old faith, the old pride
Wherein our fathers died,
Whereby our land was builded and dignified.

Toussaints

(To J. W. H.)

Like softly clanging cymbals were
Plane-trees, poplars Autumn had
Arrayed in gloriously sad
Garments of beauty wind-astir;
It was the day of all the dead—

Toussaints. In sombre twos and threes
Between those coloured pillars went
Drab mourners. Full of presences
The air seemed . . . ever and anon rent
By a slow bell's solemnities.

The past year's gloriously dead
Came, folk dear to that rich earth
Had given them sustenance and birth,
Breath and dreams and daily bread,
Took labour-sweat, returned them mirth.

Merville across the plain gleamed white,
The thronged still air gave never a sound,
Only, monotonous untoned
The bell of grief and lost delight.
Gay leaves slow fluttered to the ground.

Sudden, that sense of peace and prayer
Like vapour faded. Round the bend
Swung lines of khaki without end. . . .
Common was water, earth and air;
Death seemed a hard thing not to mend.

The Stone-breaker

(To Dorothy)

The early dew was still untrodden,
    Flawless it lay on flower and blade,
The last caress of night's cold fragrance
    A freshness in the young day made.

The velvet and the silver floor
    Of the orchard-close was gold inlaid
With spears and streaks of early sunlight—
    Such beauty makes men half afraid.

An old man at his heap of stones
    Turned as I neared his clinking hammer,
Part of the earth he seemed, the trees,
    The sky, the twelve-hour heat of summer.

"Fine marnen, zür!" And the earth spoke
    From his mouth, as if the field dark red
On our right hand had greeted me
    With words, that grew tall grain instead.

.   .   .

Oh, years ago, and near forgot!
    Yet, as I walked the Flemish way,
An hour gone, England spoke to me
    As clear of speech as on that day;

Since peasants by the roadway working
    Hailed us in tones uncouth, and one
Turned his face toward the marching column,
    Fronted, took gladness from the sun.

And straight my mind was set on singing
    For memory of a wrinkled face,
Orchards untrodden, far to travel,
    Sweet to find in my own place.

Drifting Leaves

The yellow willow leaves that float
   Down Severn after Autumn rains
Take not of trouble any note—
   Lost to the tree, its joys and pains.

But man that has a thousand ties
   Of homage to his place of birth,
Nothing surrenders when he dies;
   But yearns for ever to his earth—

Red ploughlands, trees that friended him,
   Warm house of shelter, orchard peace.
In day's last rosy influence dim
   They flock to us without a cease;

Through fast-shut doors of olden houses
   In soundless night the dear dead come,
Whose sorrow no live folk arouses,
   Running for comfort hither home.

Though leaves on tide may idly range,
   Grounding at last on some far mire—
Our memories can never change:
   We are bond, we are ruled with Love's desire.

Contrasts

If I were on the High Road
   That runs to Malvern Town,
I should not need to read, to smoke,
   My fear of death to drown;
Watching the clouds, skies, shadows dappling
   The sweet land up and down.

But here the shells rush over,
    We lie in evil holes,
We burrow into darkness
    Like rabbits or like moles,
Men that have breathed the Severn air,
    Men that have eyes and souls.

To-day the grass runs over
    With ripples like the sea,
And men stand up and drink air
    Easy and sweet and free;
But days like this are half a curse,
    And Beauty troubles me.

The shadows under orchards there
    Must be as clear and black—
At Minsterworth, at Framilode—
    As though we had all come back;
Were out at making hay or tedding,
    Piling the yellow stack.

The gardens grow as freshly
    On Cotswold's green and white;
The grey-stone cottage colours
    Are lovely to the sight,
As we were glad for dreams there,
    Slept deep at home at night;

While here we die a dozen deaths
    A score of times a day;
Trying to keep up heart and not
    To give ourselves away.
"Two years longer," "Peace to-morrow,"
    "Some time yet," they say!

To F. W. H.

Ink black and lustreless may hold
  A passion full of living fire:
Spring's green the Autumn does enfold—
  Things precious hide their bright in the mire.

And a whole country's lovely pride
  In one small book I found that made
More real the pictured Severn side
  Than crash and shock of cannonade.

Beneath, more strong than that dread noise
  The talk I heard of trees and men,
The still low-murmuring Earth-voice . . .
  God send us dreams in peace again.

The Immortal Hour

(To Winnie)

I have forgotten where the pleasure lay
  In resting idle in the summer weather,
Waiting on Beauty's power my spirit to sway,
  Since Life has taken me and flung me hither;

Here where gray day to day goes dully on,
  So evenly, so grayly that the heart
Not notices nor cares that Time is gone
  That might be jewelled bright and set apart.

And yet, for all this weight, there stirs in me
  Such music of Joy when some perceivéd flower
Breaks irresistible this crust, this lethargy,
  I burn and hunger for that immortal hour

When Peace shall bring me first to my own home,
    To my own hills; I'll climb and vision afar
Great cloud-fleets line on line up Severn come,
    Where winds of Joy shall cleanse the stain of war.

To his Love

He's gone, and all our plans
    Are useless indeed.
We'll walk no more on Cotswold
    Where the sheep feed
    Quietly and take no heed.

His body that was so quick
    Is not as you
Knew it, on Severn river
    Under the blue
    Driving our small boat through.

You would not know him now ...
    But still he died
Nobly, so cover him over
    With violets of pride
    Purple from Severn side.

Cover him, cover him soon!
    And with thick-set
Masses of memoried flowers—
    Hide that red wet
    Thing I must somehow forget.

Migrants
(To Mrs Taylor)

No colour yet appears
On trees still summer fine,
The hill has brown sheaves yet,
Bare earth is hard and set;
But autumn sends a sign
In this as in other years.

For birds that flew alone
And scattered sought their food
Gather in whirring bands;—
Starlings, about the lands
Spring cherished, summer made good,
Dark bird-clouds soon to be gone.

But above that windy sound
A deeper note of fear
All daylight without cease
Troubles the country peace;
War birds, high in the air,
Airplanes shadow the ground.

Seawards to Africa
Starlings with joy shall turn,
War birds to skies of strife,
Where Death is ever at Life;
High in mid-air may burn
Great things that trouble day.

Their time is perilous,
Governed by Fate obscure;
But when our April comes
About the thatch-eaved homes,—
Cleaving sweet air, the sure
Starlings shall come to us.

Old Martinmas Eve

The moon, one tree, one star.
Still meadows far,
Enwreathed and scarfed by phantom lines of white.
November's night
Of all her nights, I thought, and turned to see
Again that moon and star-supporting tree.
If some most quiet tune had spoken then;
Some silver thread of sound; a core within
That sea-deep silentness, I had not known
Ever such joy in peace, but sound was none—
Nor should be till birds roused to find the dawn.

After Music

Why, I am on fire now, and tremulous
    With sense of Beauty long denied; the first
    Opening of floodgate to the glorious burst
Of Freedom from the Fate that limits us
To work in darkness pining for the light,
    Thirsting for sweet untainted draughts of air,
    Clouds sunset coloured, Music . . . O Music's bare
White heat of silver passion fiercely bright!
While sweating at the foul task, we can taste
    No Joy that's clean, no Love but something lets
    It from its power; the wisest soul forgets
What's beautiful, or delicate, or chaste.
Orpheus drew me (as once his bride) from Hell.
If wisely, her or me, the Gods can tell.

The Target

I shot him, and it had to be
One of us! 'Twas him or me.
"Couldn't be helped," and none can blame
Me, for you would do the same.

My mother, she can't sleep for fear
Of what might be a-happening here
To me. Perhaps it might be best
To die, and set her fears at rest.

For worst is worst, and worry's done.
Perhaps he was the only son . . .
Yet God keeps still, and does not say
A word of guidance any way.

Well, if they get me, first I'll find
That boy, and tell him all my mind,
And see who felt the bullet worst,
And ask his pardon, if I durst.

All's a tangle. Here's my job.
A man might rave, or shout, or sob;
And God He takes no sort of heed.
This is a bloody mess indeed.

Twigworth Vicarage

(To A. H. C.)

Wakened by birds and sun, laughter of the wind,
    A man might see all heart's desire by raising
    His pillowed sleepy head (still apt for lazing
And drowsy thought)—but then a green most kind

Waved welcome, and the rifted sky behind
   Showed blue, whereon cloud-ships full-sailed went
      racing,
   Man to delight and set his heart on praising
The Maker of all things, bountiful-hearted, kind.

May Hill, the half-revealéd tree-clad thing,
   Maisemore's delightful ridge, where Severn flowing
   Nourished a wealth of lovely wild things blowing
      Sweet as the air—Wainlodes and Ashleworth
To northward showed, a land where a great king
      Might sit to receive homage from the whole earth.

Hospital Pictures

(To the Nurses of Ward 24,
Bangour War Hospital, near Edinburgh)

1. LADIES OF CHARITY

With quiet tread, with softly smiling faces
   The nurses move like music through the room;
While broken men (known, technically, as "cases")
   Watch them with eyes late deep in bitter gloom,
As though the Spring were come with all the Graces,
   Or maiden April walked the ward in bloom.

Men that have grown forgetful of Joy's power,
And old before their time, take courtesy
So sweet of girl or woman, as if some flower
Most strangely fair of Spring were suddenly
Thick in the woods at Winter's blackest hour—
The gift unlooked for—lovely Charity.

Their anguish they forget, and, worse, the slow
Corruption of Joy's springs; now breathe again
The free breath was theirs so long ago.
Courage renewed makes mock at the old pain.
Life's loveliness brings tears, and a new glow.
Somehow their sacrifice seems not in vain.

2. DUST

Lying awake in the ward
Long hours as any must,
I wonder where the dust
Comes from, the Dust, the Dust!
That makes their life so hard,—
The nurses, who must rub
The soon appearing crust
Of green on the bright knob.

And little bits of fluff,
Dull white upon the floor,
Most soft, most curious stuff
That sidles to the door
When no one sees, and makes
Deep wrinkles and heart-breaks;
Light sighs and curses rough.

Oh! if a scientist
Of warm and kindly heart
Should live a while apart,
(Old Satan's tail to twist,)
Poring on crucibles,
Vessels uncanny, till
He won at last to Hell's
Grand secret of ill-will—
How Fluff comes and how Dust,

Then nurses all would paint
Cheeks pretty for his sake;
Or stay in prayer awake
All night for that great Saint
Of Cleanliness, that bright
Devoted anchorite;
Brave champion and true knight.

3. "ABERDONIAN"

A soldier looked at me with blue hawk-eyes,
With kindly glances sorrow had made wise,
And talked till all I'd ever read in books
Melted to ashes in his burning looks;
And poets I'd despise and craft of pen,
If, while he told his coloured wonder-tales
Of Glasgow, Ypres, sea mist, spouting whales
(Alive past words or power of writing men),
My heart had not exulted in his brave
Air of the wild woodland and sea wave;
Or if, with each new sentence from his tongue,
My high-trumphing spirit had not sung
As in some April when the world was young.

4. COMPANION—NORTH-EAST DUG OUT

He talked of Africa,
    That fat and easy man.
I'd but to say a word,
    And straight the tales began.

And when I'd wish to read,
    That man would not disclose
A thought of harm, but sleep;
    Hard-breathing through his nose.

Then when I'd wish to hear
　　More tales of Africa,
'Twas but to wake him up,
　　And but a word to say

To press the button, and
　　Keep quiet; nothing more;
For tales of stretching veldt,
　　Kaffir and sullen Boer.

O what a lovely friend!
　　O quiet easy life!
I wonder if his sister
　　Would care to be my wife. . . .

5. THE MINER

Indomitable energy controlled
By Fate to wayward ends and to half use,
He should have given his service to the Muse,
To most men shy, to him, her humble soldier,
Frank-hearted, generous, bold.

Yet though his fate be cross, he shall not tire
Nor seek another service than his own:
For selfless valour and the primal fire
Shine out from him, as once from great Ulysses,
That king without a throne.

6. UPSTAIRS PIANO

O dull confounded Thing,
You will not sing
Though I distress your keys
With thumps; in ecstasies

Of wrath, at some mis-said
Word of the deathless Dead!

Chopin or dear Mozart,
How must it break your heart
To hear this Beast refuse
The choice gifts of the Muse!
And turn your airy thought
With clumsiness to nought.

I am guilty too, for I
Have let the fine thing by;
And spoilt high graciousness
With a note more or less;
Whose wandering fingers know
Not surely where they go;
Whose mind most weak, most poor,
Your fire may not endure
That's passionate, that's pure.

And yet, and yet, men pale
(Late under Passchendaele
Or some such blot on earth)
Feel once again the birth
Of joy in them, and know
That Beauty's not a show
Of lovely things long past.

And stricken men at last
Take heart and glimpse the light,
Grow strong and comforted
With eyes that challenge night,
With proud-poised gallant head,
And new-born keen delight.

Beethoven, Schumann, Bach:
These men do greatly lack,

And you have greatly given.
The fervent blue of Heaven
They will see with purer eyes—
Suffering has made them wise;
Music shall make them sweet.

If they shall see the stars
More clearly after their wars,
That is a good wage.
Yours is a heritage
Most noble and complete.
And if we, blind, have gone
Where a great glory shone.
Or deaf, where angels sang;
Forgive us, for you, too,
A little blind were, knew
Of weakness, once, the pang;
Of darkness, once, the fear.

And so, forgive this dear
Pig-hearted chest of strings,
And me, whose heart not sings
Nor triumphs as do yours
Within the Heavenly doors—
Walking the clear unhindered level floors.

Hidden Tales

The proud and sturdy horses
Gather their willing forces,
Unswerving make their courses
Over the brown
Earth that was mowing meadow
A month agone, where shadow
And light in the tall grasses
Quivered and was gone.

They spoil the nest of plover
And lark, turn up, uncover
The bones of many a lover
Unfamed in tales;
Arrows, old flints of hammers,
The rooks with hungry clamours
Hover around and settle
Seeking full meals.

Who knows what splendid story
Lies here, what hidden glory
Of brave defeat or victory
This earth might show.
None cares; the surging horses
Gather untiring forces
The keen-eyed farmer after
Guiding the plough.

Recompense

(To the Men of the 2/5 Gloucester Regiment)

I'd not have missed one single scrap of pain
That brought me to such friends, and them to me;
And precious is the smallest agony,
The greatest, willingly to bear again—
Cruel frost, night vigils, death so often ta'en
By Golgothas untold from Somme to Sea.
Duty's a grey thing; Friendship valorously
Rides high above all Fortune without stain.

Their eyes were stars within the blackest night
Of Evil's trial. Never mariner
Did trust so in the ever-fixéd star
As I in those. And so their laughter sounded—

Trumpets of Victory glittering in sunlight;
Though Hell's power ringed them in, and night
    surrounded.

The Tryst

(To W. M. C.)

In curtain of the hazel wood,
    From sunset to the clear-of-star,
An hour or more I feared, but stood—
    My lover's road was far.

Until within the ferny brake
    Stirred patter feet and silver talk
That set all horror wide awake—
    I fear the fairy folk . . .

That bind with chains and change a maid
    From happy smiling to a thing
Better in ground unhallowed laid
    Where holy bells not ring.

And whether late he came or soon
    I know not, through a rush of air
Along the white road under the moon
    I sped, till the golden square

Showed of the blind lamplighted; then,
    My hand on heart, I slackened, stood . . .
Though Robin be the man of men,
    I'll walk no more that wood.

The Plain

The plain's a waste of evil mire,
  And dead of colour, sodden-grey,
The trees are ruined, crumbled the spire
  That once made glad the innocent day.

The host of flowers are buried deep
  With friends of mine who held them dear;
Poor shattered loveliness asleep,
  Dreaming of April's covering there.

Oh, if the Bringer of Spring does care
  For Duty valorously done,
Then what sweet breath shall scent the air!
  What colour-blaze outbrave the sun!

Rumours of Wars

(To Mrs Voynich)

On Sussex hills to-day
  Women stand and hear
The guns at work alway,
  Horribly, terribly clear.

The doors shake, on the wall
  The kitchen vessels move,
The brave heart not at all
  May soothe its tortured love,

Nor hide from truth, nor find
  Comfort in lies. No prayer
May calm. All's naught. The mind
  Waits on the throbbing air.

The frighted day grows dark.
    None dares to speak. The gloom
Makes bright and brighter the spark
    Of fire in the still room.

A crazy door shakes free. . . .
    "Dear God!" They stand, they stare . . .
A shape eyes cannot see
    Troubles blank darkness there.

She knows, and must go pray
    Numb-hearted by the bed
That was his own alway . . .
    The throbbing hurts her head.

"On Rest"

(To the Men of the 2/5 Gloucester Regiment)

It's a King's life, a life for a King!
To lie safe sheltered in some old hay-loft
Night long, on golden straw, and warm and soft,
Unroused; to hear through dreams dawn's thrushes sing
"Revally"—drowse again; then wake to find
The bright sun through the broken tiles thick-streaming.
"Revally" real: and there's an end to dreaming.
"Up, Boys, and Out!" Then O what green, what still
Peace in the orchard, deep and sweet and kind,
Shattered abruptly—splashing water, shout
On shout of sport, and cookhouse vessels banging,
Dixie against dixie musically clanging.—
The farmer's wife, searching for eggs, 'midst all
Dear farmhouse cries. A stroll: and then "Breakfast's up."
Porridge and bacon! Tea out of a real cup
(Borrowed). First day on Rest, a Festival

Of mirth, laughter in safety, a still air.
"No whizzbangs," "crumps" to fear, nothing to mind,
Danger and the thick brown mud behind,
An end to wiring, digging, end to care.
Now wonders begin, Sergeants with the crowd
Mix; Corporals, Lance-Corporals, little proud,
Authority forgotten, all goes well
In this our Commonwealth, with tales to tell,
Smokes to exchange, letters of price to read,
Letters of friends more sweet than daily bread.
The Sergeant-major sheathes his claws and lies
Smoking at length, content deep in his eyes.
Officers like brothers chaff and smile—
Salutes forgotten, etiquette the while,
Comrades and brothers all, one friendly band.
Now through the orchard (sun-dried of dewfall) in
And out the trees the noisy sports begin.
He that is proud of body runs, leaps, turns
Somersaults, hand-turns; the licensed jester flings
Javelins of blunt wit may bruise not pierce;
Ragtimes and any scrap of nonsense sings.
All's equal now. It's Rest, none cares, none escapes
The hurtless battering of those kindly japes.
Noon comes, the estaminets open welcome doors,
Men drift along the roads in three and fours,
Enter those cool-paven rooms, and sit
Waiting; many there are to serve, Madame
Forces her way with glasses, all ignores
The impatient clamour of that thirsty jam,
The outcries, catcalls, queries, doubtful wit,
Alike. Newspapers come, "Journal, m'sieur?"
"What's the news?" "Anything fresh, boy?"
   "Tell us what's new."
Dinner, perhaps a snooze, perhaps a stroll.
Tea, letters (most like), rations to divide
(Third of a loaf, half, if luck's our way).
No work, no work, no work! A lovely day!

Down the main street men loiter side by side.
So day goes on blue-domed till the west's afire
With the sun just sunken, though we cannot see,
Hidden in green, the fall of majesty.
Our hearts are lifted up, fierce with desire
But once again to see the ricks, the farms,
Blue roads, still trees of home in the rich glow;
Life's pageant fading slower and more slow
Till Peace folds all things in with tender arms.
The last stroll in the orchard ends, the last
Candles are lit in bivvy and barn and cart,
Where comrades talking lie, comfort at heart,
Gladder for danger shared in the hard past,
The stars grow bright 'gainst heaven's still-deepening
    blue,
Lights in the orchard die. "I wonder how
Mother is keeping: she must be sleepy now
As we, yet may be wondering all night through."

Dicky

(To His Memory)

They found him when the day
Was yet but gloom;
Six feet of scarréd clay
Was ample room
And wide enough domain for all desires
For him, whose glowing eyes
Made mock at lethargies,
Were not a moment still;—
Can Death, all slayer, kill
The fervent source of those exultant fires?
Nay, not so;
Somewhere that glow

And starry shine so clear astonishes yet
The wondering spirits as they come and go.
Eyes that nor they nor we shall ever forget.

Omiecourt

The Day of Victory

(To my City)

The dull dispiriting November weather
Hung like a blight on town and tower and tree,
Hardly was Beauty anywhere to see
Save—how fine rain (together
With spare last leaves of creepers once showed wet
As it were, with blood of some high-making passion,)
Drifted slow and slow. . . .
But steadily aglow
The City was, beneath its grey, and set
Strong-mooded above the day's inclemency.

Flaunting from houses, over the rejoicing crowd,
Flags waved; that told how nation against nation
Should war no more, their wounds tending awhile:—
The sullen vanquished; Victors with heads bowed.
And still the bells from the square towers pealed Victory,
The whole time cried Victory, Victory flew
Banners invisible argent; Music intangible
A glory of spirit wandered the wide air through.
All knew it, nothing mean of fire or common
Ran in men's minds; none so poor but knew
Some touch of sacred wonder, noble wonder,—
Thought's surface moving under;
Life's texture coarse transfiguring through and through.

Joking, friendly-quarrelling, holiday-making,
Eddying hither, thither, without stay
That concourse went, squibs, crackers, squibbing,
    cracking—
Laughter gay
All common-jovial noises sounded, bugles triumphing
    masterful, strident, clear above all,
Hail fellow, cat-call . . .
Yet one discerned
A new spirit learnt of pain, some great
Acceptance out of hard endurance learned
And truly; wrested bare of hand from Fate.
The soldier from his body slips the pack,
Staggers, relaxes, crouches, then lies back,
Glad for the end of torment. Here was more.

A sense of consummation undeserved,
Desire fulfilled beyond dreams, completion
Humbly accepted,—a proud and grateful nation
Took the reward of purpose had not swerved;
But steadily before
Saw out, with equal mind, through alternation
Of hope and doubt—a four-year purge of fire
Changing with sore
Travail the flawed spirit, cleansing desire.

And glad was I:
Glad—who had seen
By Somme and Ancre too many comrades lie.
It was as if the Woman's spirit moved
That multitude, never of Man that pays
So lightly for the treasure of his days—
Of some woman that too greatly had beloved
Yet, willing, half her care of life foregone;
Best half of being losing with her son,
Beloved, beautiful, born-of-agony One. . . .

The dull skies wept still. Drooped suddenly
Flags all. No triumph there.
Belgium, the Stars and Stripes, Gaul, Italy,
Britain, assured Mistress, Queen of the Sea,
Forlorn colours showed; rags glory-bare.
Night came, starless, to blur all things over
That strange assort of Life;
Sister, and lover,
Brother, child, wife,
Parent—each with his thought, careless or passioned,
Of those who gave their frames of flesh to cover
From spoil their land and folk, desperately fashioned
Fate stubborn to their will.

Rain fell, miserably, miserably, and still
The strange crowd clamoured till late, eddied,
        clamoured,
Mixed, mused, drifted. . . . The Day of Victory.

Passionate Earth

(To J. W. H.)

Where the new-turned ploughland runs to clean
Edges of sudden grass-land, lovely, green—
Music, music clings, music exhales,
And inmost fragrance of a thousand tales.
There the heart lifts, the soul takes flight to sing
High at Heaven-gate; but loth for entering
Lest there such brown and green it never find;
Nor feel the sting
Of such a beauty left so far behind.

The Poplar

(To Micky)

A tall slim poplar
    That dances in
A hidden corner
    Of the old garden,
What is it in you
    Makes communion
With this wind of Autumn
    The clouds, the sun?

You must be lonely
    Amidst round trees
With their matron-figures
    And stubborn knees,
Casting hard glances
    Of keen despite
On the lone girl that dances
    Silvery white.

But you are dearer
    To sky and earth
Than lime-trees, plane-trees
    Of meaner birth.
Your sweet shy beauty
    Dearer to us
Than tree-folk, worthy,
    Censorious.

Down Commercial Road (Gloucester)

(To my Mother)

When I was small and packed with tales of desert islands
    far
  My mother took me walking in a grey ugly street,
But there the sea-wind met us with a jolly smell of tar,
  A sailorman went past to town with slow rolling gait;
    And Gloucester she's famous in story.

The trees and shining sky of June were good enough to
    see,
  Better than books or any tales the sailormen might
    tell—
But tops'le spars against the blue made fairyland for me;
  The snorting tug made surges like the huge Atlantic
    swell.
    And Gloucester she's famous in story.

Then thought I, how much better to sail the open seas
  Than sit in school at spelling-books or sums of
    grocers' wares.
And I'd have knelt for pity at any captain's knees
  To go see the banyan tree or white Arctic bears.
    And Gloucester she's famous in story.

O Gloucester men about the world that dare the seas
    to-day,
  Remember little boys at school a-studying their best
To hide somehow from Mother, and get clear away
  To where the flag of England flies prouder than the rest.
    And Gloucester she's famous in story.

From Omiecourt

O small dear things for which we fight—
    Red roofs, ricks crowned with early gold,
    Orchards that hedges thick enfold—
O visit us in dreams to-night!

Who watch the stars through broken walls
    And ragged roofs, that you may be
    Still kept our own and proudly free
While Severn from the Welsh height falls.

Le Coq Français

(To Ronald)

After the biting cold of the outer night
It seemed—("Le Coq Français")—a palace of light,
And its low roof black-timbered was most fine
After the iron and sandbags of the line.
Easy it was to be happy there! Madame,
Frying a savoury mess of eggs and ham,
Talking the while: of the War, of the crops, her son
Who should see to them, and would, when the War was
    done.
Of battalions who had passed there, happy as we
To find a house so clean, such courtesy
Simple, sincere; after vigils of frost
The place seemed the seventh Heaven of comfort; lost
In miraculous strange peace and warmth we'd sit
Till the prowling police hunted us out of it—
Away from café noir, café au lait, vin blanc,
Vin rouge, citron, all that does belong
To the kindly shelter of old estaminets,
Nooked and cornered, with mirth of firelight ablaze—

Herded us into billets; where candles must show
Little enough comfort after the steady glow
Of that wonderful fireshine. We must huddle us close
In blankets, hiding all but the crimson nose,
To think awhile of home, if the frost would let
Thought flow at all; then sleep, sleep to forget
All but home and old rambles, lovely days
Of maiden April, glamorous September haze,
All darling things of life, the sweet of desire—
Castles of Spain in the deep heart of the fire.

The Fisherman of Newnham

(To my Father)

When I was a boy at Newnham,
　For every tide that ran
Swift on its way to Bollo,
　I wished I were a man
To sail out and discover
　Where such a tide began.

But when my strength came on me
　'Tis I must earn my bread:
My Father set me fishing
　By Frampton Hock, instead
Of wandering to the ocean—
　Wherever Severn led.

And now I've come to manhood,
　Too many cares have I
To think of gallivanting
　(A wife and child forbye).
So I must wonder ever
　Until time comes to die.

Then I shall question Peter
   Upon the heavenly floor,
What makes the tide in rivers—
   How comes the Severn bore,
And all things he will tell me
   I never knew before.

The Lock-keeper

(To the Memory of Edward Thomas)

A tall lean man he was, proud of his gun,
Of his garden, and small fruit trees every one
Knowing all weather signs, the flight of birds,
Farther than I could hear the falling thirds
Of the first cuckoo. Able at digging, he
Smoked his pipe ever, furiously, contentedly.
Full of old country tales his memory was;
Yarns of both sea and land, full of wise saws
In rough fine speech; sayings his father had,
That worked a twelve-hour day when but a lad.
Handy with timber, nothing came amiss
To his quick skill; and all the mysteries
Of sail-making, net-making, boat-building were his.
That dark face lit with bright bird-eyes, his stride
Manner most friendly courteous, stubborn pride,
I shall not forget, not yet his patience
With me, unapt, though many a far league hence
I'll travel for many a year, nor ever find
A winter-night companion more to my mind,
Nor one more wise in ways of Severn river,
Though her villages I search for ever and ever.

The Revellers

I saw a silver-bright shield hang
Entangled in the topmost boughs
Of an old elm-tree, and a house
Dreaming; the while a small stream sang
A tune of broken silver by,
And laughed and wondered at the sky.

A thousand thousand silver lamps
Dared the bright moon of stars. O! who,
Wandering that silver quiet through,
Might heed the river-mists, dew-damps?
All Heaven exulted, but Earth lay
Breathless and tranced in peace alway.

From the orange-windowed tavern near
A song some ancient lover had—
When stars and longing made him mad—
Fashioned from wonder at his dear,
Rang out. Yet none there moves a limb
To see such stars as passioned him.

The loth moon left the twigs and gazed
Full-fronted at the road, the stream,
That all but tiniest tunes adream
Stilled, held breath at last amazed.
The farmers from their revel came;
But no stars saw, and felt no flame.

"Annie Laurie"

(To H. N. H.)

The high barn's lit by many a guttering flare
    Of flickering candle, dangerous—(hence forbidden)—

To warm soft straw, whereby the cold floor's hidden,
On which we soon shall rest without a care.
War is forgotten. Gossip fills the air
    Of home, and laughter sounds beyond the midden
    Under the stars, where Youth makes Joy unchidden
Of gods or men, and mocks at sorrow there.
But hark! what sudden pure untainted passion
    Seizes us now, and stills the garrulous?
A song of old immortal dedication
        To Beauty's service and one woman's heart.
    No tears we show, no sign of flame in us
        This hour of stars and music set apart.

The Battalion is Now on Rest

(To "La Comtesse")

Walking the village street, to watch the stars and find
Some peace like the old peace, some soothe for soul and
        mind;
The noise of laughter strikes me as I move on my way
Towards England—Westward—and the last glow of day.

And here is the end of houses. I turn on my heel,
And stay where those voices a moment made me feel
As I were on Cotswold, with nothing else to do
Than stare at the old houses, to taste the night-dew;

To answer friendly greetings from rough voices kind. . . .
Oh, one may try for ever to be calm and resigned,
A red blind at evening sets the poor heart on fire—
Or a child's face, a sunset—with the old hot desire.

Photographs

(To Two Scots Lads)

Lying in dug-outs, joking idly, wearily;
  Watching the candle guttering in the draught;
Hearing the great shells go high over us, eerily
  Singing; how often have I turned over, and laughed

With pity and pride, photographs of all colours,
  All sizes, subjects: khaki brothers in France;
Or mother's faces worn with countless dolours;
  Or girls whose eyes were challenging and must dance,

Though in a picture only, a comon cheap
  Ill-taken card; and children—frozen, some
(Babies) waiting on Dicky-bird to peep
  Out of the handkerchief that is his home

(But he's so shy!). And some with bright looks, calling
  Delight across the miles of land and sea,
That not the dread of barrage suddenly falling
  Could quite blot out—not mud nor lethargy.

Smiles and triumphant careless laughter. O
  The pain of them, wide Earth's most sacred things!
Lying in dugouts, hearing the great shells slow
  Sailing mile-high, the heart mounts higher and sings.

But once—O why did he keep that bitter token
  Of a dead Love?—that boy, who, suddenly moved,
Showed me, his eyes wet, his low talk broken,
  A girl who better had not been beloved.

That County

Go up, go up your ways of varying love,
    Take each his darling path wherever lie
    The central fires of secret memory;
Whether Helvellyn tower the lakes above;
Or black Plinlimmon time and tempest prove;
    Or any English heights of bravery.
    I will go climb my little hills to see
Severn, and Malverns, May Hill's tiny grove.

No Everest is here, no peaks of power
    Astonish men. But on the winding ways
    White in the frost-time, blinding in full June blaze,
    A man may take all quiet heart's delight—
Village and quarry, taverns and many a tower
    That saw Armada beacons set alight.

Interval

To straight the back, how good; to see the slow
    Dispersed cloud-flocks of Heaven wandering blind
    Without a shepherd, feel caress the kind
Sweet August air, soft drifting to and fro
Meadow and arable.—Leaning on my hoe
    I searched for any beauty eyes might find.
    The tossing wood showed silver in the wind;
Green hills drowsed wakeful in the golden glow.

Yet all the air was loud with mutterings,
    Rumours of trouble strange in that rich peace,
    Where War's dread birds must practise without cease
    All that the stoutest pilot-heart might dare.
Death over dreaming life managed his wings,
    Droning dull song in the sun-satiate air.

De Profundis

If only this fear would leave me I could dream of
    Crickley Hill
  And a hundred thousand thoughts of home would
    visit my heart in sleep;
But here the peace is shattered all day by the devil's will,
  And the guns bark night-long to spoil the velvet
    silence deep.

O who could think that once we drank in quiet inns and
    cool
  And saw brown oxen trooping the dry sands to slake
Their thirst at the river flowing, or plunged in a silver
    pool
  To shake the sleepy drowse off before well awake?

We are stale here, we are covered body and soul and
    mind
  With mire of the trenches, close clinging and foul,
We have left our old inheritance, our Paradise behind,
  And clarity is lost to us and cleanness of soul.

O blow here, you dusk-airs and breaths of half-light,
  And comfort despairs of your darlings that long
Night and day for sound of your bells, or a sight
  Of your tree-bordered lanes, land of blossom and
    song.

Autumn will be here soon, but the road of coloured
    leaves
  Is not for us, the up and down highway where go
Earth's pilgrims to wonder where Malvern upheaves
  That blue-emerald splendour under great clouds of
    snow.

Some day we'll fill in trenches, level the land and turn
  Once more joyful faces to the country where trees
Bear thickly for good drink, where strong sunsets burn
  Huge bonfires of glory—O God, send us peace!

Hard it is for men of moors or fens to endure
  Exile and hardship, or the Northland grey-drear;
But we of the rich plain of sweet airs and pure,
  Oh! Death would take so much from us, how should
    we not fear?

The Tower

(To M. H.)

On the old road of Roman, on the road
Of chivalry and pride—the path to Wales
Famed in the chronicles and full of tales—
Westward I went, songs in my mouth, and strode
Free-bodied, light of heart,
Past many a heaped waggon with golden load,
And rumbling carrier's cart.
When, near the bridge where snorting trains go under
With noise of thunder,
I turned and saw
A tower stand, like an immortal law—

Permanent, past the reach of Time and Change,
Yet fair and fresh as any flower wild blown;
As delicate, as fair
As any highest tiny cloudlet sown
Faint in the upper air.
Fragile yet strong, a music that vision seemed.
Though all the land was fair, let the eye range
Whither it will

On plain or hill,
It must return where white the tower gleamed
Wonderful, irresistible, bubble-bright
In the morning light.
And then I knew, I knew why men must choose
Rather the dangerous path of arms than let
Beauty be broken
That is God's token,
The sign of Him; why hearts of courage forget
Aught but the need supreme
To follow honour and the perilous thing;
Scorning Death's sting;
Knowing Man's faith not founded on a dream.

COMMENTARY

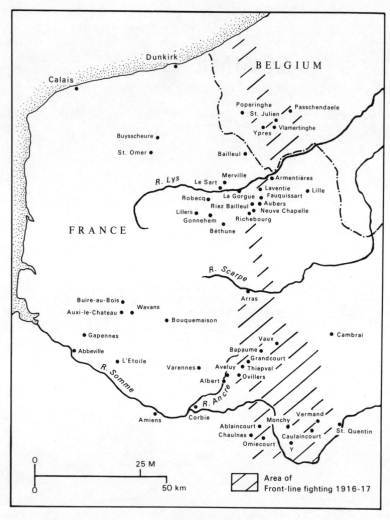

Gurney's France, 1916–17

THE COMPOSITION OF
Severn & Somme

In a letter of 5 July 1916, Gurney wrote from the Front to Marion Scott to ask for a "penny manuscript book or some MS in the parcel" (*WL* 82). On the 7 August he complained that "You send me an exercise book, which may yet contain my Collected Poems. But it was music M.S. I meant" (*WL* 90). In spite of the small number of poems that Gurney by then had written, both he and Marion Scott were turning their minds to collecting together his poems for publication, and there was the beginning of that splitting of the creative stream into poetry as well as music. Although Gurney was to write that "if there is a whole after-the-war for me, little enough verse will I write again—most, *most* probably, I know which is my chief game" (*WL* 127), he was never to pause for long in his flood of creative writing.

Marion Scott had proposed sending a sonnet (probably "To England—A Note") to the *Westminster* before 17 July 1916 (GA 41.31), and from this almost joking reference to publication the idea began to take on a definite shape, and writing was to become the prop in the army that it was later to be in the asylum. The project required pressure both from Gurney and from Marion Scott and he was always warm in his tributes to her: "I doubt whether it would have been written but for you" (*WL* 177), he wrote when the book was nearing publication.

The first serious proposal comes in a letter of 19 October 1916 where he writes that "At present I have it in my mind to write 15 or 20 more, and chiefly of local interest, make a book, and call it 'Songs from the Second-Fifth'" (GA 41.43). By the 17 January 1917 it seemed a fixed project:

Really, the book has filled up lately, n est ce pas? And if they give me but a little time in the Batt: to myself; or if the nice Blighty comes along; or if the spring weather comes and finds me rejoicing in it—the Complete Opus 1 of my Poetical Works (or will it be "Poetical Remains"?) will be on view. What is the minimum required? Please tell me; for if there had not been this mean definite end in view, I doubt whether I should have written above a couple of things this last month. So queerly are we made! (GA 41.54).

But just the day after this, he writes both confidently and hesitantly. His letter of 18 January 1917 (*WL* 118–20) ends "Book progressing plenty bon?" but does not seem quite so confident earlier. In a passage which stresses the importance of the book as yet another connection with the ubiquitous F. W. Harvey, Gurney asks

> Would you mind telling me candidly sincerely as possible, what you think of my things were they collected in a book and compared to FWH's? Personally, I think there is nothing of mine so good as "Flanders". And also, perhaps, "If we return", but outside those, I think my things are better on the whole and more poetical. Do you think there is too much regret in mine? His book has a fine spirit, is mine too much the confession of being unwillingly a soldier? Is there too much of a whine? I would not be out of it—right out of it—for anything; this gives me a right to talk and walk with braver men than myself and an insight into thousands of characters and a greater Power over Life, and more Love.

This comes in a letter which includes his "Song: Only the Wanderer" and accompanies his setting of "In Flanders".

Hesitant or not, Gurney agreed with Marion Scott very soon afterwards that Sidgwick and Jackson would be the best publishers to approach; they had after all published Harvey's book which was always a model, implicitly if not explicitly, just as Harvey was the presiding presence in Gurney's book. Plans proceded; in a letter posted on 21 January 1917, he is writing of what poems to include, how he will make the arrangement, and announcing that "There will also be a Preface" (*WL* 122). On 14 February he writes that "The first poem will be To Certain Comrades; the last poems, the five sonnetts. . . . And mix up things as you please" (*WL* 131). The Preface was prepared by 15 February (*WL* 133–4), and in February

Marion Scott sent a list of poems on which Gurney wrote a suggested title and dedicated various poems to various individuals; but by 5 March the publishers had still not been approached.

On 30 April 1917, encouraged by what he saw as poor writing in the *Poetry Review*, Gurney was writing to Marion Scott to "Please rush my book into print as soon as possible" (*WL* 159). She sent him a list of the poems she had and he numbered them "chiefly by size" (GA 41.92) and returned the list on 13 May. This list is substantially what was printed although there are differences. Gurney deleted at this stage "Robecq", "Song: Ah! tell me not the spirits of the trees", "Poor Folk", and "February Day"; the three poems called "Requiem" are not numbered for inclusion nor deleted; and the list does not include "Letters", "Strafe", "Spring. Rouen, May 1917", "Song at Morning", or the final sonnet of "Sonnets 1917"; "Sawgint", "The Colonel" and "Dawn" were deleted later at the suggestion of the publisher.

On 9 June 1917, F. Sidgwick of Sidgwick and Jackson wrote to T. F. Dunhill, hoping that Marion Scott would send Gurney's manuscript soon and noted on the same letter that she had done so (GA 61.258); there is a receipt form from the firm for *Strange Service*. Dunhill, with whom Marion Scott had contacts through the Royal College of Music, had obviously acted as intermediary. Sidgwick replied immediately: "Should we publish, I think it probable that we should like to suggest several alterations in the MS., as we did for 'A Gloucestershire Lad'. . . . May I add that, speaking for myself, I agree with Mr. Dunhill that Mr. Gurney's work is of great interest and promise, though it lacks the easy and lyrical simplicity of Mr. Harvey; and this latter characteristic has doubtless helped the popularity of 'A Gloucestershire Lad'. I do not think 'Strange Service' would achieve a similar success. But that is not to say that we necessarily refuse to publish it" (GA 61 259–60). In July, Gurney was anxious about the lack of progress and was telling Marion Scott that "I remember Harvey had trouble with S and Js, and had to tickle them up" (*WL* 175); but on the 14 July, she sent him a telegram "Sidgwick will publish your book" (GA 41.124). The telegram reached him just about the same time as he was told that he had been attached to a machine gun company and he wrote of a "crowded half-hour of glorious life" (*WL* 176). Marion Scott then conducted a complicated three-way discussion with Gurney and S and J's editor R. B. McKerrow about contracts and royalties. The contract proposed and eventually agreed in spite of objections gave 10% on all copies sold after the first 500 and up to 2,000, 15% from 2,000 to 10,000 and 25% thereafter; "No royalty to accrue on the first 500" it said ominously (GA 61.261), though McKerrow explained this was normal for verse. Gurney would have liked an advance, and could "not see why the book should not pay" (*WL* 178), but he left the arrangements in Scott's hands and wrote to the publisher giving her authority to deal with them in his behalf (GA 41.116).

It was in these discussions that the final selection was made. McKerrow suggested removing "The Colonel", "Sawgint", and thought that "Song and Pain", "The Dawn", and "Communion" were "hardly up to the general level of the book" (GA 61.263–4). Gurney wanted to keep "Sawgint" because of its subject, but "'Communion' I am fond of and think that S and Js are wrong" (GA 41.114). He offered alternatives which appear in the book. The book was set in proof and Gurney eagerly anticipated the job of correcting them: "A double set of proofs! Yum. Yum!!" (GA 41.128). He received them "the day before I went sick" of gas, and corrected them in the hospital, expecting to rejoin his machine gun unit. On the 21 September he sent them back to Marion Scott, wishing that he were worse and could have got to Blighty (*WL* 200). On the 22 September he sailed back to England.

There was a further alteration to be made in the book, since the Press Bureau, who acted as censors for printed books, refused to allow the mention of the numbers 2/5 in connection with the Gloucesters. With the acquiescence that the cover be red (*WL* 223) his influence on the book ended.

Four strands running throughout the making of the book deserve some brief mention, however: the name of the book, its punctuation, corrections, and dedications.

As I mentioned above, "Songs from the Second-Fifth" was the first idea for a title, but in a letter of 18 January 1917 he began to see that "It is doubtful whether the book, if book it comes to be, can ever have for title 'Songs of the Second-Fifth', since there is so little of the battallion in it" (*WL* 118). He tried other names: "Songs from Exile, or Songs from the Second Fifth" on 14 February (*WL* 129); or "Songs in Exile" in another letter posted the same day; even "Songs of Exile and other Songs" in a list of poems of late February (GA 70.1). Marion Scott obviously told him that there already was a book with that title, so in March he offered "Remembered Beauty" or "Beauty Remembered" or "Songs before Dawn" (*WL* 140). In May he was trying "To Certain Comrades and other Verses" (*WL* 161). He plumps for "Severn & Somme" in a letter of 4 June 1917: "The title 'Severn and Somme' might sell the book a little better. It sounds like a John Bull poster, but otherwise there is nothing objectionable about it. Severn people may buy if Somme people don't: my French not being equal to translation of works so delicate of language" (*WL* 165). Marion Scott however chose "Strange Service" which, says Gurney, "is a very exact description of the feeling that made the book; it would sell better as 'Severn and Somme' perhaps, but that is your business" (*WL* 179). It was as "Strange Service" that the book was submitted to Sidgwick and Jackson but McKerrow agreed with Gurney and in a letter of 27 July 1917 suggested the change to the title we know, *Severn & Somme* (GA 61.263–4).

On the matter of punctuation, Gurney is casual, feeling there are more urgent matters to occupy his attention; which is why I have not felt it to be worthwhile to record punctuation changes in this edition, and have felt it reasonable to make some slight punctuation changes in the quotations. He often told Marion Scott to punctuate for him: "Now I have reached your corrections of my punctuation, and approve" (8 October 1916, *WL* 105); "punctuate as you please, and take no notice of any marks of mine" (14 February 1917, *WL* 131; see also 10 March, GA 41.70; and 20 March, GA 41.77). None the less, he does insist on his own "correctness" of grammar: "The grammar of my book is, technically speaking, often shaky. Never poetically. I say what I want to say" (*WL* 141).

There is a continuous process of correction taking place in the correspondence between Gurney and Marion Scott. He would send her a poem or sometimes an exercise book full of poems. She would ask questions, make comments, and later transcribe them and send them for correction. Sometimes she would make a correction which he would accept while disagreeing with it, as in the case of "To Certain Comrades" or "To the Poet before Battle". To account for all of these changes would entail reprinting large amounts of the letters, so I have noted only some of the changes in the notes.

Perhaps the question that seems to cause Gurney most agony is that of the dedications. Apart from the dedication of the book to Margaret Hunt, and those poems like "To Certain Comrades" and "After-Glow", where the dedication is part of the title, Gurney plays with dedications: allocates a poem to someone, forgets the dedication, allocates it to someone else, and finally despairs of it all. Except for poems explicitly in memory of someone, or to Harvey, poems were usually allocated on a basis of association or because a particular individual might like a poem. So, in spite of organising dedications to many of the poems, he decided on 13 August to tell Marion Scott to "delete *all* dedications save three—'To Certain Comrades'; and one each to yourself and F. W. H." (*WL* 185). But later in August, "O those damned dedications!" (GA 41.126) and on the 27th "I think it will be better to omit nearly all dedications, because (1) People will begin to compare. (2) It looks silly and makes the book a sort of family affair. Yes, I would prefer them out" (GA 41.128). Despite all this, on 24 November 1917, he prepared a list of dedications for the second edition, not all of them agreeing with the dedications proposed for the first edition. The whole business of dedications seems to belong to Gurney's emotional but difficult relations with people which reflects the commitments of his poetry; but since they are incidental to that poetry and were finally omitted, I have not resurrected them.

Severn & Somme was published in mid-November 1917 at two shillings and sixpence. In a letter postmarked 17 November 1917 he reports that the "notices of my book were out yesterday" (*WL* 230), and the reviews were favourable. In the *Telegraph* it was said that "There is the authentic voice of the true poet in Ivor Gurney". Gurney thought *The Times* review "charming, I think; and satisfactory, save for the stress laid on my being a 'Gloucestershire' poet" (GA 70.12.1). He continued: "I did not expect Osborne to be pleased with my book for he is a Prussian—still, his treatment of my book is all I could expect; and his reference to my double endings pleased me very much". E. B. Osborne had reviewed the book for the *Morning Post* under the title "A Voluntary" and is a shrewd observer. He makes the connection with Harvey and Gloucestershire, and sees the connection with music: "But the musician comes out, not so much in explicit notes of this kind, as in the subtle avoidance of all jog-trot, this-way-to-market, rhythms and in the artistic management of vowel-sounds, and in the use of the diminished double rhyme (honour . . . manner . . . praises . . .

faces, and so on), all of which gives his verse an air of distinction even when he has had no time to polish it" (GA 61.76). The last comment in the review is prophetic, if indeed it did not help to create the later verse: "I shall look eagerly for the poems he will weave out of War's passion in retrospect when this storm is over-past."

According to Gurney's contacts in London, "Harvey's two books, a 'Shropshire Lad' and mine are selling like hot cakes" (*WL* 234) late in November, though it was not out of print as he reported it. It is impossible to say how many were sold since the size of the print run is not known, but McKerrow reported to Marion Scott on 15 January 1919 that "at Christmas we came almost to the end of the first impression of 'Severn and Somme' and are now reprinting" (GA 61.272). A royalty statement for the second half of 1918 (GA 61.270) shows royalties on 33 copies (seven shillings and sevenpence!), which indicates that sales had exceeded 500 copies and that the sales had been largely in the first months after the book's publication. Royalty statements in the Gurney Archive (GA 11.2) are incomplete, but indicate a sale of both Gurney's books in ones and twos throughout the twenties and thirties, until there is a boost into over thirty copies of each in the half year immediately following his death.

It only remains to say what Gurney thought of his book. From time to time he writes of his aims and opinions. On 23 February 1917, he wrote:

What I want to do with this book is

(1) To leave something definite behind if I am knocked out
(2) To say out what Gloucester is, and is to me; and so to make Gloucester people think about their county
(3) To have *some* good stuff in it, whatever one might say about the whole
(4) To make people realise a little what the ordinary life is.

Anyway it was good fun, writing; and gave me something to do. (*WL* 137)

He always recognised its shortcomings in technique: "simple lack of energy ... kept me from revision, and the only method possible to me was to write for a minute or two at top speed, refrain from tearing it up, and return to the charge after some space of time"

115

(*WL* 160). Lack of energy, lack of opportunity and lack of time are recurring themes, as is the comparison of the book with Harvey's; but the most sustained account of his views comes in a letter where he comments on the terms agreed for payment and reflects on why he wrote:

> My own opinion of the book is, that it is very interesting, very true, very coloured; but its melody is not sustained enough, its workmanship rather slovenly, and its thought, though sincere, not very original and hardly ever striking. For all that, the root of the matter is there, and scraps of pure beauty often surprise one; there is also a strong dramatic sense. Where it will fail to attract is that there is none, or hardly any of the devotion to self-sacrifice, the splendid readiness for death that one finds in Grenfell, Brooke, Nichols, etc. That is partly because I am still sick of mind and body, partly for physical, partly for mental reasons; also because, though I am ready if necessary to die for England, I do not see the necessity; it being only a hard and fast system which has sent so much of the flower of England's artists to risk death, and a wrong materialistic system; rightly or wrongly I consider myself able to do work which will do honour to England. Such is my patriotism and I believe it to be the right kind. (*WL* 178)

His opinions vary from dispassionate dismissal—"outside the one line 'Fragile mirrors easily broken by moving airs', I do not recall any line of real beauty" (*WL* 184)—to a sense of dismay: "Why, O why did I, did I write . . ." (*WL* 191); but they also include a solid sense of its worth: "Of course the technique is rough, but the book is sincere and interesting and original. I never claimed more" (GA 41.92). One might claim more, but one could not claim less.

NOTES TO
Severn & Somme

In Gloucester Public Library there is a second impression of *Severn & Somme* annotated by Ivor Gurney probably in the asylum period. In it he noted the places where each poem was written; in the following notes this is referred to as SSIG; MMS is Marion Scott, GA the Gurney Archive, and *WL* is *Ivor Gurney War Letters*.

The book was dedicated to Margaret Hunt.

PREFACE, p. 19
Ms in a letter of 15 February 1917 (*WL* 133–4)—obviously copied from a draft, as two words were missed out in the copying (see the letter of 5 March 1917; *WL* 141); but the whole sentence about roughness of technique and all the next sentence up to "Gloucester" were missing. Perhaps they derive from the more combative end to the Preface offered in a letter of 18[?] May 1917 (GA 41.93):

> All the verses ... two or three earlier pieces. This should be reason enough to excuse the roughness of the technique, and if more reason is required by the Critical Master of Words (who is rightly angry at clumsiness and botched work) or the Arty Quibbler, (may he be poleaxed!) I would say, that it is my Royal Pleasure that it should remain rough—this book; with all its imperfections on its head. Say, O Quibbler, could You write with an empty belly and various internal disturbances? Not You; your exquisitely chiselled phrases need a velvet jacket and a crowd of imbeciles to bring them forth. Just go to Ablaincourt next November and have a look at it. (Don't forget your pack.) You people of home, and, most of all, you people of Gloucester, may well be indulgent etc.
> And then at the end
> And if you *won't* be indulgent—why, dammy, I can do without you! I shall survive. though not as a poet perhaps.

The change from "5 Platoon, B Co, 2/5 Glosters" to "my comrades of two platoons of the -/- Gloucesters", and of "the Second-Fifth" to "the Gloucesters" was demanded by the Press Bureau, who were the censors for printed books (see letter from R. B. McKerrow to MMS of 26 September 1917; GA 61.268–9). Located at Buire au Bois in SSIG.

TO CERTAIN COMRADES, p. 21
Ms in "Literary Supplement" to letter to MMS of 5 July 1916 (*WL* 83) where it was called "To the Fallen (E. S.)"; the title was changed in a letter of August 1916 (*WL* 92). l.3 is corrected from the original confusing "And though our spirits had in high in honour". l.9 changes the initial word from "Nor" to "And", since Gurney was horrified by "Nor" when it appeared in the *RCM Magazine* as if he had not written it (See *WL* 104). The Ms corrected "far" in l.11 to "grey", but the printed version reverts to the original. In the Ms, l.17 begins "How ended! and the aching hearts" although Gurney seems surprised by the "very trite schoolboy alteration of the second All ended to How ended!" (*WL* 98). l.21 began originally "That such an ending as yours" which Gurney defends in a letter of early August 1916 on the grounds that it crescendos at "yours" rather than having "portion" as climax (GA 70.4); but he accepts the correction later (*WL* 98). Located at Fauquissart in SSIG.

Published in the *RCM Magazine* Vol 12, No. 3, Midsummer Term 1916. There is a typescript in a group of poems by Gurney published in periodicals collected by J. W. Haines (GA 66.1). Gurney's letter of 14 February 1917 (*WL* 131) says nothing about the order of the book except that this poem will be the first and the five sonnets the last. Two soldiers of the 2/5 Gloucesters with these initials who died shortly before 5 July 1916 were Pte E Skillern and Pte J Hall; the fact that they died in action on the same day—21 June 1917—and that they are buried three graves apart in a cemetery at Laventie makes the identification certain.

THE FIRE KINDLED, p. 22
I have not located a Ms but the poem was written in October 1916. There are four transcripts, three of the draft version and one of the version as printed. GA 52.11.172 is a copy by MMS; GA 64.11.26–7 is a transcript by MMS with the date "October 1916" deleted; GA 64.11.29–30 is a transcript in another hand without the deletion. It is from one of these texts that the version in the *RCM Magazine* was set up. Gurney was horrified when he saw it: "What the Constellation of Orion has Bellows' compositor or the censor done to my poor poor 'Fire Kindled'? [. . .] God help me, I meant no such thing. What has happened to my Heine-ending? Did it reach you too illegible, or was I mad, or have I unconsciously altered it since?" (GA 41.58). He revised it then and there, explaining that

"God" (not "O God") in the first line is "a *swear* not a *prayer*". The last stanza had ended:

> But not by Gloster willows . . .
> Dreams, dreams and useless dreams.

In a second letter posted the same day, 3 February 1917, he completed his revision by rewriting stanza 3 (GA 41.55). The fourth transcript by MMS, GA 64.11.28, incorporates the revisions and adds the note "(2nd version.) Jan 1917".

Gurney mentions the poem in a letter of 15 December 1916 (*WL* 114–5), defending the line "How hot my heart desires" and saying he only remembered the end "which was that poem's reason for being"; and nearly a year later, on 16 October 1917 he declared that "The things I should most like to write are things of beauty with a vinegary ending, something after 'The Fire Kindled'. Heine I believe is famous for that sort of thing" (*WL* 222). Located at Merville in SSIG.

TO THE POET BEFORE BATTLE, p. 23
Ms in letter of 3 August 1915. Probably the first of his poems sent to MMS, and in a letter where he writes of Rupert Brooke (*WL* 34–5); written before he left England; SSIG locates this in Chelmsford. The fourth line was changed at MMS's suggestion from "Unstirred by the tattle and rattle of rolling drums". Gurney accepted the alteration but added "I do not understand the objection to it though" (*WL* 48). The poem was printed in the *RCM Magazine*, Vol 12, No 1, Christmas Term 1915, and there is a typescript in J. W. Haines's collection of Gurney poems published in periodicals (GA 66.1).

MAISEMORE, p. 23
Ms in envelope dated 8 November 1916 (GA 41.46). MMS transcribed the poem (GA 64.11.31–2) and sent another copy to Gurney, which he revised, particularly stanza 4, and returned on 20 March 1917 (GA 41.77). SSIG locates this "E of Laventie".

AFTERWARDS, p. 24
Ms in letter of September 1915 (*WL* 35 ff), line 12 corrected on 23 February 1917 (*WL* 137), replacing "Then the sad heart" with "The troubled heart". MMS objected to "Maybe" in line 9, but Gurney defended the use of the word (*WL* 48). The poem was printed in the *RCM Magazine* Vol 12, No 1, Christmas Term 1915. There is a typed copy in J. W. Haines's collection of Gurney poems published in periodicals (GA 66.2). Located by SSIG at Chelmsford.

CAROL, p. 25
Ms in letter of 19 November 1915 (*WL* 47). SSIG locates this in Chelmsford. In a letter of 5 March 1917, Gurney calls it "merely pretty" but wishes to include it to dedicate to Micky Chapman (Marjorie; see *Stars In a Dark Night*, ed Anthony Boden).

STRANGE SERVICE, p. 26
Ms in letter of 27 July 1916 (*WL* 87–8). MMS transcribed it and Gurney corrected her transcript (GA 52.11.105). He thought of calling it "Dreams and Action" (19 October 1916; GA 41.43 and 41.44). At one point "Strange Service" was thought of as a title for the whole book. SSIG locates this poem at Tilleloy and adds "Written on same day as 'By a Bierside'".

SERENITY, p. 27
Ms in letter to Mrs Voynich of 28 August 1916 (*WL* 100) where first lines are "Nor flame nor steel has any power on me,/ But that its power work the Almighty Will." Gurney wrote that "I note the two 'powers'; but perfection is not a thing I value, but only Truth and Beauty" (*WL* 100). He made the alteration in a letter to Mrs Voynich of September 1916 (GA 41.36) and sent the corrected version to MMS on 10 October 1916 (*WL* 108). He returned her fair copy unmarked on 20 March 1917 (GA 41.77). He headed it "Rondel (is it?)" on 28 August; on 25 October he says it was "meant for a triolet—but I know none of the forms" (*WL* 110). It has the limitation to two rhymes and the line repetition, but is a line short of a standard triolet. Gurney would have been familiar in his much-loved *The Spirit of Man* with Julian Grenfell's "Into Battle", with its lines:

Nor lead nor steel shall reach him, so
    That it be not the Destined Will.

SSIG locates this simply "Trenches". See also under 'COMMUNION'.

THE SIGNALLER'S VISION, p. 27
Ms in envelope dated 8 November 1916 (GA 41.46). Gurney was made a signaller in May 1916. In a letter to MMS of 29 March 1917, written sitting in the midst of soldiers and writing of the prospect of his poems being shown to Robert Bridges, Gurney says that "things like the 'Signaller's Vision' are meant to appeal to such people as are in this room with me—not the experimenters in Greek metres" (*WL* 146). SSIG locates this "Trenches E of Laventie".

THE MOTHER, p. 28
Ms in letter of 30 November 1916 to MMS (GA 41.47). It follows this

passage: "I saw a perfectly lovely wood the other day, and beyond it, what I should take to be a fine specimen of an old camp—which would be difficult to take today. How horrible to have written that last sentence about a beautiful ridge of earth!" When MMS sent it to Gurney for correction in a letter to which he replied on 17 January 1917, he had forgotten it: "I never remembered seeing it before, until next day; when the memory of an impromptu came to me—it was merely part of a letter, and went clean out of my mind when it was sent" (GA 41.54). SSIG locates this E of Laventie.

TO ENGLAND—A NOTE, p. 28
Ms in letter to MMS of 29 June 1916 (*WL* 79) transcribed by MMS and corrected in letter of 5 March 1917 (GA 41.71). Gurney removes a little of the overstrained "poetic" by changing "mire" to "water" in the second line and removes something of the anti-German feeling by revising the 10th line from "The flood of German beastliness so long". The song referred to in the last lines is "I want to go home", which he had reported to MMS on 22 June 1916 was "The Song that Signallers Sung and Stretcherbearers of C Company, when the great guns roared at them, and the Germans thought to attack" (*WL* 75). SSIG locates this both in Laventie and Tilleloy.

BACH AND THE SENTRY, p. 29
Ms in envelope dated 8 November 1916 (GA 41.46). Probably in relation to this poem, Gurney wrote to MMS on 4 March 1917 "to answer a query—I have no certain Dearest Prelude. Perhaps the E major 1st book (*my* arrangement—NOT Bach's) or the C major or G minor or A♭ or F major from the 2nd Book . . . Surely the 48 is the wisest of all the works of man? It trains one like the noble touch of Pain; yet who could understand Bach without having suffered?" (*WL* 140). SSIG locates this variously "Laventie Aubers E of Laventie".

LETTERS, p. 29
There is a pencil draft of this poem in GA 52.7, a red notebook used at the front. The first draft was much more concerned with the war:

Mail's up, the height of all desiring,
The silent trench begins to buzz;
The patient sniper ceases firing.
Mail's up, the height of all desiring.
And all's forgotten of the tiring
Night, as long as Egypt's was.

Gurney copied the second draft in a group headed "Rondels" in a letter of

11 June 1917 to MMS (*WL* 169). Her transcription of it is at GA 64.11.34. Located E of Laventie by SSIG.

STRAFE, p. 29
Also in the red notebook (GA 52.7), sent in letter of 11 June 1917 to MMS (*WL* 170) and transcribed by her (GA 64.11.33). Located E of Laventie by SSIG.

ACQUIESCENCE, p. 30
Ms in envelope dated 8 November 1916 (GA 41.46). In l.13 "can" was altered from "could" in a letter of 23 March 1917 (*WL* 144). Located E of Laventie by SSIG.

THE STRONG THING, p. 30
Ms in letter of 22 December 1916 to MMS (GA 41.50). Located E of Laventie by SSIG.

SCOTS, p. 31
Ms in envelope dated 4 January 1917 (GA 41.52). Gurney was always enthusiastic about people with a distinctive identity. In a letter of 27 December 1916, he writes: "As for the Scots—O it is a joy to meet the water-cart drivers and attendants of the 51st division. The Scots are certainly the finest of races" (GA 41.51). On 7 January 1917, he reported that "I made my fastest friendship on record with two Scots Engineers lately" and reports on their singing of Scottish folksong; and on New Year's Eve the pipers playing "We've been happy a' thegither" (GA 41.53). Marion Scott was enthusiastic and Gurney replied on 17 January that " 'Scots' seems to have been quite a success; since there is no sort of incident connected with me that brought it out—it was the talk and tales of the men who won the victory in November (was it?)" (GA 41.54). In a letter of 24 November 1917, Gurney comments on the printed text and wishes to "alter the last line of 'Scots' " to coincide with the last lines of the earlier stanzas (GA 41.158). Located at Crucifix Corner in SSIG.

TO AN UNKNOWN LADY, p. 31
Ms in letter of 22 December 1916 to MMS (GA 41.50). Gurney defends his lines in a letter of 7 January 1917 (GA 41.53) and says the unknown lady is "but a figment or a dream of passion". Located "near Somme" by SSIG.

SONG AND PAIN, p. 32
Ms in letter of 7 January 1917 to MMS (GA 41.53) along with "Purple and Black" and "Communion". In a letter of 21 January 1917 Gurney said

that "it surprises me that you like 'Song and Pain' best. It seems the least of those three" (*WL* 121). Located at Crucifix Corner by SSIG.

PURPLE AND BLACK, p. 32
Ms in letter of 7 January 1917 (GA 41.53). Located E of Laventie by SSIG.

WEST COUNTRY, p. 33
Ms in letter of 18 January 1917 (*WL* 119–20). Having copied this out, Gurney comments that "All these lispings of childhood do not prevent terrific strafing on the left, where Hell is apparently combined with the angry gods to make things thoroughly uncomfortable". Located E of Laventie by SSIG.

FIRELIGHT, p. 34
Ms in letter of 3 February 1917 (*WL* 125). Gurney emended "thrills with music" to "thrills and murmurs" in stanza two (*WL* 147). The letter transcribing the poem treats it ironically by adding immediately after it "But O, cleaning up!" Gurney had been recently reading Yeats enthusiastically and the effect shows in the last stanza. Located at Varennes by SSIG.

THE ESTAMINET, p. 34
Ms in letter of 17 January 1917 to MMS (GA 41.54), where he offers in parenthesis above the title "Noctes ambrosianae? or Deorum?". Gurney's opinion may be deduced from his comment to MMS that "The prophet must always be annoyed when a friend tells him how much better slippers and a churchwarden become him than the splendid mantle, and so your sister's liking for the 'Estaminet' does not please me" (*WL* 167), though he later wrote that "I am not sure she is not right about liking 'Estaminet' best" (*WL* 207). "Minnies" were minenwerfers or trench mortars. Located at Arras by SSIG.

SONG, p. 36
Ms in letter of 18 January 1917 to MMS (*WL* 119). Gurney offered and wisely rejected the alternative "Who loves fair Joy as he" for line 5. The fact that Gurney transcribes this poem just after mentioning F. W. Harvey may well indicate an association with him and his poems, particularly "Flanders", which begins "I'm homesick for my hills again" and which Gurney admired sufficiently to transcribe more than once. Located at Coulaincourt by SSIG.

BALLAD OF THE THREE SPECTRES, p. 36
Ms in letter of 15 February 1917 (*WL* 134) along with the Preface.

Gurney comments "Not so bad eh?" He asked in a later letter "Is it Border-Ballady?" (23 February 1917, GA 41.66). Located "Somme" by SSIG.

COMMUNION, p. 37
Ms in letter of 7 January 1917 to MMS (GA 41.53). In a letter of 17 January 1917, Gurney wrote: "I am very interested to know what you think of 'Communion', which seems to me to be one of the most successful of all, if not, with 'Serenity', the most successful" (GA 41.54). Located at Crucifix Corner by SSIG.

TIME AND THE SOLDIER, p. 38
Ms in letter of 21 January 1917 to MMS (*WL* 121); Ms of the last three stanzas in an undated letter to Mrs Voynich is probably earlier (GA 41.61). In a letter of early February 1917, Gurney thought this poem "will improve on you: it is W. H. Davies, but stronger; and one of my best" (*WL* 127). Located at Crucifix Corner by SSIG.

INFLUENCES, p. 38
Ms in letter of 21 January 1917 to MMS (*WL* 121–2). Located E of Laventie by SSIG.

AFTER-GLOW (To F. W. Harvey), p. 39
Ms in letter of 9 February 1917 to MMS (GA 41.67); another Ms dated "Jan 1917" in letter of 23 February 1917 to MMS (*WL* 138). Writing of the last line of the poem in another letter of 23 February 1917 to MMS, Gurney asked "What do you think of the substitution of 'firelight' for 'music'? It seems to be the more full of point—to sum up the beauty of afterglow and firelight too; does not Bach's music do so?" (GA 41.66). Gurney thought a lot about Harvey. The previous August he had feared for a while that Harvey was dead: "F.W.H. is almost certainly dead, and with him my deepest friendship, as far as that does pass with death; a very little with me" (*WL* 94). By October he knew that Harvey was well though in prison, and in January he was wondering how his poems would compare with Harvey's if collected in a book. In the letter which contains the later Ms of this poem he writes:

> I wonder how FWH has got on in prison lately … My thoughts of England are first and foremost of the line of Cotswold ending with Bredon Hill, near Tewkesbury, and seen with him. Or the blue Malverns seen at a queer angle, from the hayfield, talking when War seemed imminent, and the whole air seemed charged with fateful beauty (*WL* 137).

Located at Varennes by SSIG.

HAIL AND FAREWELL, p. 40

Ms in letter of 3 February 1917 to MMS (GA 41.59). In the first line "The destined bullet" replaces "A German bullet". This poem "stands pretty high" in Gurney's opinion on 9 February 1917 (GA 41.67). Located E of Laventie by SSIG.

PRAISE, p. 40

Ms in letter of 23 February 1917 to MMS (*WL* 139). Located E of Laventie by SSIG.

WINTER BEAUTY, p. 41

Ms in letter of 9 February 1917 to MMS (GA 41.67) on a sheet of paper splashed with stain from a bully-beef tin exploding in the raging fire before which Gurney is writing. But "these two disgracefully dirty scraps of paper I am sending contain two of my best things". It is there called "Beauty" and Gurney says he has taken "quite a lot of trouble" about it. This Ms version lacks the third stanza. The first stanza changes substantially;

> I cannot live with Beauty out of mind.
> I search for her and desire her all the day,
> Beauty, the choicest treasure man may find,
> Most joyous and sweetest word his lips can say.
> The crowded heart in me is quick with visions
> And sweetest music born of a brighter day.

Gurney's revisions and the addition of the third stanza which make up the printed version are written in a letter of 14 August 1917 and dated "Jan–Aug 1917 (GA 41.120). In a letter to Herbert Howells of early February 1917, Gurney thinks that Howells will like lines 11–12 (GA 3.29) and a typed transcript of the poem, which derives from the 3-stanza version, is dedicated to H. N. Howells (GA 64.11.2). In a note of 24 November 1917, Gurney comments that the printed text should delete the final s of "consolations" in l.12 (GA 41.158). Located at Verennes in SSIG.

SONGS OF PAIN AND BEAUTY, p. 42

Ms in letter of 7 March 1917 to MMS (*WL* 142). Gurney says he is "rather proud" of these verses (letter of 29 March 1917, *WL* 146) and that "I believe the long line in the Song of Pain and Beauty is quite all right. It is like 3/4 after 2/4" (*WL* 148). The poem was printed in the *RCM Magazine*, Vol 13, No 3, Midsummer Term 1917, and thus appears in

J. W. Haines's typed copies of poems printed in periodicals (GA 66.4). Located at Gommecourt and at Chaulnes by SSIG, with the annotation "Frosted finger, written lying on soaked sandbags".

SPRING. ROUEN, MAY 1917, p. 42

A substantial part of Gurney's Red Notebook (GA 52.7) is taken up with pencil drafts of this poem, with much crossing out but the final poem clearly emerging. Two points are worth making from the many revisions there: first that it seems at one point as if it is to be addressed to "Dear Willy" (i.e. Harvey again); second that there seemed to be a rounding of the subject back to the blackbirds of the opening, with an indication of Gurney's hopes of returning to England because of his wound; after the words which end the printed poem, he writes:

> We shall grow free at heart and great and young
> You shall return (the Blackbird sang)
> Safe over sea
> Safe in the nest that sheltered you of old
> Cool in the sultry time, warm in the cold
> O think no bitter thoughts of France and me
> Safe oversea.

He transcribes the poem in a letter of 24 May 1917 to MMS (GA 41.95) with the comment "There is some more of this; would you like to have it? At any rate it will fill up." On 11 June, Gurney wrote that he had read some poems to a friend and found them remote; "As for Spring 1917, it is as I thought long, dull, and unvaried" (*WL* 170). In a letter of 21 August 1917, having seen his book in print and compared it with two books he received at the same time, he asks "Why the Ruddy Hades did I write 'Spring 1917'?" (*WL* 191). Gurney was in a hospital at Rouen in May 1917 wounded by a bullet that "went clean through the right arm just underneath the shoulder"; but because the hospital boats were held up he lost his "chance for Blighty" (*WL* 154). SSIG locates this, not surprisingly, at Rouen.

JUNE-TO-COME, p. 45

Ms in letter of 22 March 1917 to MMS (GA 41.72) where it is dedicated to F.W.H. Located at Arras by SSIG.

"HARK, HARK, THE LARK", p. 46

Ms in letter of 22 March 1917 to MMS (GA 41.72) where it is dedicated to F.W.H. The opening phrase is quoted from Shakepeare's song in *Cymbeline* act II scene iii. The prison, and the Cloucester nostalgia connect the poem strongly with Harvey. Located at Arras by SSIG, which also includes a development of "Fear no more the heat of the sun".

SONG AT MORNING, p. 47
There is a pencil draft in the Red Notebook (GA 52.7), but this is unfinished, ending after a version of ll 17–18: "Though I in Hell, self's stubborn hell would shut me / Resentful and most proud!". A letter dated 27 June 1917 to MMS reports he is glad she likes it, as she has said in a letter of the 23rd. She made a fair copy which agrees with the printed text (GA 64.11.35–6). In a letter of 29 September 1917 to MMS, written from the Edinburgh Military Hospital at Bangour and thus not subject to censorship, Gurney could be precise about places: he was "in the line for 8 days at Arras, to the right of Monchy, watching which hill-village at dawn, I thought of the 'Song at Morning'" (*WL* 209). This corresponds with the comment in a letter written on about 8 June 1917 that "We have been in the line or thereabouts for over a week" (GA 41.98). Annotated in SSIG "Arras Dawn written guess June 1917 Looking at it".

TREES, p. 48
The prose is an extract from a letter of 10 March 1917 to MMS (GA 41.70) written after Gurney's longest spell in the trenches. Ms of the poem is in a letter of 22 March 1917 to MMS (GA 41.72); here the second stanza differs greatly:

Where Cooper's stands by Cranham
And grey stone houses smile,
Where motion, joy-inspired,
Eats up the measured mile.

The revised version is given in a letter of 18[?] May 1917 to MMS (GA 41.93). Gurney has had most difficulty with the third stanza, where he has arrived at the final version of its last two lines after deleting "Most lovely Gloster-worthy/ And then I, fool, O Fool". Located at Arras by SSIG.

REQUIEM: "Pour out your light", p. 48
Ms in envelope dated 8 November 1916 (GA 41.46).

REQUIEM: "Nor grief nor tears", p. 49
Ms in envelope dated 8 November 1916 (GA 41.46). Located E of Laventie by SSIG.

REQUIEM: "Pour out your bounty", p. 49
Ms in envelope dated 8 November 1916 (GA 41.46).

Sonnets 1917

This group of sonnets is a deliberate reply to Rupert Brooke and should be read with an eye on his poems. Gurney wrote that "These Sonnetts, For England, Pain, Homesickness, Servitude, and one other; are intended to be a sort of counterblast against 'Sonnetts 1914', which were written by an officer (or one who would have been an officer). They are the protest of the physical against the exalted spiritual; of the cumulative weight of small facts against the one large. Of informed opinion against uninformed (to put it coarsely and unfairly) and fill a place. Old ladies won't like them, but soldiers may, and these things are written either for soliders or civilians as well informed as the French what 'a young fresh war' means. (Or was it 'frische (joyful) Krieg'. I can't remember, but something like it was written by a tame German in 1914.) I know perfectly well how my attitude will appear, but—They will be called 'Sonnetts 1917'" (*WL* 130).

1. FOR ENGLAND, p. 49
Ms in envelope sent to MMS and dated 13 February 1917 (GA 41.74). In letter of 9 February 1917 to MMS, Gurney writes that "The next sonnet I shall work on has for Octett, thoughts on the loveliness of life, and for Sestett, how, if one must leave these things, then a death in arms for England is not so bad. That shall say all I think, and it shall stand last in my book" (GA 41.67). A letter of 7 March 1917 to MMS suggests an alteration which was not taken up for the second quatrain (GA 41.76):

> Where never the late bird is heard to sing ...
> And (or for) England's image must indeed be slow
> To fade. How shall dull her sombre glow
> Of Autumn sunsets, or the fire of Spring?

2. PAIN, p. 50
Ms in a letter of February 1917 to MMS (*WL* 128), where there is a rough draft, a fair copy with no verbal difference from the printed version, and Gurney's comment: "Which is also an impromptu—the first of Sonnetts 1917, 5 of them, for admirers of Rupert Brooke. They will make good antitheses; but the note of the rest will be quite different; this being the blackest" (*WL* 128). Gurney alters little from the rough draft. Located "Somme or Crucifix Corner" by SSIG.

3. SERVITUDE, p. 50
Ms in letter of 14 February 1917 to MMS (*WL* 130). In 1.13 "Hell-fire" replaces the original "Bosches". Gurney had the soldiers' ambivalence about the Germans: "In the mind of all the English soldiers I have met there is absolutely no hate for the Germans, but a kind of brotherly

though slightly contemptuous kindness" (*WL* 136). Located at Arras by SSIG.

4. HOME-SICKNESS, p. 51

Ms in letter of 14 February 1917 to MMS (*WL* 129). Located at Arras by SSIG.

5. ENGLAND THE MOTHER, p. 51

Ms in letter of 29 May 1917 to MMS (GA 41.96). This was the last of the five to be written and Gurney had trouble with it. On 4 March 1917 "There are no more verses; the sonnet 'England' not having taken shape, and anyway that needs quiet and some comfort—but chiefly quiet" (*WL* 139); and on the 5th "I want to write my last sonnett, but that refuses to come, so much is there to say" (*WL* 141). On the 23rd "The sonnet to come at the end of the set will not—deposit, what is the word? (Sediment appearing from a chemical mixture.)" (GA 41.73). On the 26th "I am afraid the final sonnett does not stand a chance of getting written" (*WL* 149). On the 29th "The final sonnet seems fated not to be written; we being on short rations and hard work" (*WL* 146). After his wounding and move to Rouen "As for verse, we have been altogether too harried for me to get any calm, and anyhow I seem to have run dry. Also my inside has not been as placable as it might, though that will bring me little advantage indeed compared with my painless wound" (GA 41.86). In late April he was urging MMS to rush his book into print and saying that "If that sonnet can be done, it shall be. But continual disgust has sterilised me" (*WL* 159). Gurney's list of poems for the projected book on 13 May 1917 listed only four "Sonnets 1917" (GA 41.92). Finally on 29 May 1917, having told MMS to "do as you please about the last 1917 Sonnet", he wrote "Will this do?" and transcribed the sonnet as it was printed (GA 41.96). There is a fair copy by MMS (GA 64.11.37). Located at Arras by SSIG.

THE COMPOSITION OF
War's Embers

Before *Severn & Somme* was published, Gurney was making preparations for a second book of poems. He seems to have made a resolution to stop writing poetry, perhaps to concentrate on music, but it did not last and by 27 July 1917, well before he came back to England, he was writing: "So my resolution goes, and there probably will be another book. So look out!" (*WL* 179). In the very next letter came two poems with the comment that "this is for the next book, not this" (*WL* 181). On 13 August he was planning to make up for the lack of dedications in his first book by including them in the next "of which four masterpieces are already extant" (*WL* 185). In September he sent a notebook full of poetry to see if there was anything worth using for the new book and, with his usual optimism in this early state of creativity, asked if it would not be a better one than the first (*WL* 199). This enthusiasm is characteristically balanced by his dismissiveness in an autobiographical list he sent to Marion Scott in relation to the first book, describing himself as "Author of 'Severn and Somme' and a further unborn imbecility" (*WL* 227).

The process of writing continued as it had in France, sustaining him while in hospital in Edinburgh, on a signalling course in Seaton Delaval, in hospital in Newcastle, convalescing at Brancepeth Castle, or in hospital again in Warrington or St Albans. While at Brancepeth on 12 March 1918, he wrote that "What is happening is that my real groove lay in Nature and Music, whereas Pain and Protest forced the other book into being" and he forecast that if he went to the Front again there would be "any amount written, influenced by E T[homas] chiefly, perhaps by Robert Graves" (GA 70.20). In September 1918, Gurney sent to Marion Scott from St Albans "the precious exercise book, with its contents of 'Fairy Gold'" (GA 41.183). Obviously by this time he was able to get criticism not only from Marion Scott, but also from John Haines who could make comparisons with other poets that he knew. On 10 September 1918 Gurney reported that "Mr Haines has just sent me a long letter of criticism on the famous exercise book, so will you please return your copy for a few days, and receive it, probably with a few corrections" (GA 41.176). The Purple Exercise Book in the Gurney Archive (GA 64.9) may well be one of these copies, with its contents of a five stanza version of "The Stone Breaker" along with many other poems like "The Fisherman of Newnham", "On Rest", "Turmut-Hoeing", "Toussaints", "The Tower" and so on.

Marion Scott had not been slow in arranging things with the publisher. Soon after the publication of *Severn & Somme*, she had visited Sidgwick and Jackson. In January 1918, Gurney wrote that "Yes, you did tell me of your visit to S and Js. I am almost sure of having written about it, and their asking for my second book" (*WL* 237). But it was not until the following January that things were firmly under way. On 15 January 1919, with apologies for a delay over Christmas, R. B. McKerrow wrote to give his comments on what should be excluded from the selection he had been offered for the new book (GA 61.271).

What was submitted to him can be inferred from a draft of the title page and arrangement of poems made by Marion Scott. The title at that stage was to be "War's Bright Embers", which confirms the reference to the lines in "Camps". The arrangement of the 67 poems submitted was to be in two parts: "Part 1: Of Gloucester from France / Part 2: Of Gloucester in England" or "A 'Gloucester' in France" and "A 'Gloucester' in England / Poems / by Ivor Gurney / Private of the Gloucesters" (GA 64.11.88). Marion Scott planned out the two parts (GA 64.11.92) but submitted the poems without dividing them and with the title amended to "War's Embers". McKerrow reported back that Mr Sidgwick suggested omitting some twenty-four poems, and marked down another eight as doubtful, two of which ("The Farm" and "Fire in the Dusk") were questioned because they "suggest rather strongly a reminiscence of the work of Rupert Brooke" (GA 61.271). Gurney agreed to the omission of nine of the poems: "Ypres", "Above Ashleworth", "The Sentry", "O Tree of Pride", "Hill and Vale", "Excursion", "Question and Answer", "Triolet" and "Sundown". The rest he kept (they were "The Volunteer", "Camps", "Girl's

Song", "Day Boys and Choristers", "At Reserve Depot", "Ypres-Minsterworth", "To His Love", "Old Martinmas Eve", "Recompense", "The Plain", "Dicky", "Passionate Earth", "Down Commercial Road", "From Omiecourt", and "Interval"; and from the list of doubtfuls "The Farm", "Eternal Treasure", "Fire in the Dusk", "Solace of Men", "Toasts and Memories", "The Revellers", "Annie Laurie" and "After Music"). It is a mark of the change in taste and valuing of Gurney's work that of the nine poems which P. J. Kavanagh chose to print from the 58 in *War's Embers*, three were on McKerrow's list (including the much-praised "To His Love"), and a further three published in the section from 1917–1919 were among those excluded in agreement with the publisher's views. McKerrow also said that he slightly favoured the manuscript arrangement of the poems because "Personally I don't care much for a vol. of poetry cut up into sections and sorted".

Matters went quickly. On 25–26 February Gurney was writing to Marion Scott: "I am returning my proofs to you, with corrections from your suggestions, for which thank you very much. Some of the them had already caught my eye. Anyway here is my draft for you to do as you will with. Don't the old book read well in print though? Don't it look business-like, tight and right?" (GA 53.34). Gurney's corrected proofs are in the Gurney Archive (GA 46.26.1) along with a revise proof set annotated by Marion Scott. There was a small amount of minor alteration, but again what seemed to cause most problems was the dedications, with numerous deletions and alterations. In mid-March Gurney said that he would leave the choice of colour for the cover to Marion Scott (GA 61.6), though he added that he did like Harvey's blue covers. It was published in May, in grey covers, price three shillings.

The press was perhaps a little more critical than with his first book, although he could perhaps expect praise from F. W. Harvey, who reviewed it in the *Gloucester Journal* on 17 May 1919. Harvey commented that there is "not a bad poem in the book" and praised Gurney's "unerring sense of poetic music" but allowed himself the criticism that the poems "show a certain lack of polish, and occasional signs of hasty workmanship". The *Times Literary Supplement* of 7 August 1919 complained of Gurney's "flinging down of impressions" which makes for "good journalism. It is not poetry"; but it found a great deal of poetry and quoted "To his Love". The *Birmingham Post* of 8 July wrote that he had "no sense of the witchery of words" and advised him to study Shakespeare. In October Gurney wrote to Marion Scott: "Isn't the Birmingham critique a beauty? Still the flower of all is the Aberdonian one" (GA 46.30.5). It was not the criticism which would have tickled Gurney in the notice in the *Aberdeen Daily Journal* of 16 June 1919: the book was said to be "although above the usual run of verse, still very short of the standard of poetry" and Gurney was advised to "refrain from lapsing into literary colloquialisms"; but Gurney obviously delighted in the comment that "The author apparently voyaged in the s.s. Aberdonian, as he has a poem with that title on a Scots soldier". Sales were obviously insufficient to persuade Sidgwick and Jackson to embark on a third volume of Gurney's poems.

NOTES TO
War's Embers

In April 1925, Gurney annotated Marion Scott's copy of *War's Embers* and this is now in Gloucester Public Library. In it he recorded the places where each poem was written and at the back gave a summary of his movements during the writing of the book, carefully dated "June 1917–December 1st 1918"; in the following notes this is referred to as WEIG.

DEDICATION: TO M.M.S., p. 55
Ms in letter of 29 August 1917 to MMS (*WL* 191) dated "August 27, near P--", which may be Passchendaele, where Gurney was gassed early in September. There is a transcript by MMS (GA 64.11.64)

THE VOLUNTEER, p. 57
Ms in letter of 29 August 1917 to MMS (*WL* 192). Gurney sent MMS some corrections for poems in a Blue Exercise book (GA 52.5), which included the first two stanzas of this poem. MMS made a transcript which Gurney corrected, dated "Aug. 1917" in her hand and "Vlamer-tinghe" in his (GA 61.11.53–4). She made a fair copy of the alterations there proposed (GA 64.11.56), and a final copy incorporating all corrections (GA 64.11.144). The quotation in stanza 5 is from the end of Whitman's "Passage to India". Gurney's letter introduces the poem by saying "You will find a fresh poem below, though there is no question of volunteering", and comments "That's not so bad, I think". The poem was published in *The Spectator* of 22 February 1919, and is in J. W. Haines's collection of typescripts of poems published in periodicals (GA 66.11). Located at Edinburgh by WEIG.

THE FARM, p. 57
There is a Ms draft in the Purple Exercise Book (GA 64.9.12–13 and 19), where Gurney works out the end of the poem. It is mentioned in letter of September 1918 to MMS (GA 61.1) where he thinks it "shows pretty well now", presumably after revision. As Michael Hurd says "Gurney adopted the entire Harvey family" (*Ordeal* 24). Located at Hertford by WEIG.

OMENS, p. 59
There is a pencil rough draft of this poem in the Green Notebook (GA 64.6). Gurney rejects the more melodramatic lines like "And every note that's cried / Tells her heart how / His friend and brother died / That drove the plough" and "His letters never tell / And yet she knows" along with the more explicit parallel "They cry because their homes / Are rudely shaken"; the final form is almost there in the draft. Located at Hertford by WEIG. The dedicatee is Emily Hunt.

ETERNAL TREASURE, p. 60
Ms in letter of 24 August 1917 to MMS (GA 41.130). Gurney did not revise this and two Ms copies by MMS (GA 64.11.84 and GA 64.11.85) as well as a typed copy (GA 64.11.9) are unchanged. In the letter transcribing the poem, Gurney offers it as a poem "written between fatigues and marches and general Army worries; out of thoughts of sunset and war" and comments that "That is surely not unworthy in the Shakespearian tradition?" He dates it "V--- August 1917", which may be Vlamertinghe. In WEIG it is merely annotated "Front". The second line recalls his own "Serenity"; see p. 27. The dedicatee is Herbert Howells.

FIRE IN THE DUSK, p. 60
Ms in letter of 7 September 1918 to MMS (GA 70.43) copied from a rough draft in GA 64.5.6. Located in Gloucester by WEIG.

TURMUT-HOEING, p. 61
Gurney's Ms is dated "St Albans August 1918" (GA 64.9.17v); there is no change here, or in two transcripts by MMS (GA 64.11.57 and GA 64.11.148). Located in Hertford by WEIG.

IN A WARD, p. 62
There is a pencil draft in GA 64.5.7, from which Gurney made a copy which he dated "Warrington July" (GA 64.9.5). MMS made a copy and entered the revisions of the last two lines (GA 64.11.73). The poem was published in *The Spectator* on 11 January 1919, and J. W. Haines collected a typed copy in his poems by Gurney published in periodicals (GA 66.10). Haines is also the dedicatee. Located in Hertford by WEIG.

CAMPS, p. 63
Gurney writes to MMS on 8 August 1917 "Perhaps by now you have 'Camps' or 'Works of War', or whatever I called it" (*WL* 184), but sends another copy in a letter of 14 August 1917 (GA 41.120). He had drafted the poem in a Black Notebook (GA 52.7) which has several small differences from the final version and substantially different last stanzas:

When heaven at last her eager gates unbars
And shouts us in; I wonder shall we see
Huge ramparts and camps of those celestial wars
When Michael drew his sword of chivalry

And smote the evil power? O then we'll take
Untidy heaven in hand and make it fair
With green concealing leafage with flowers, and make
A heaven of peace even in that upper air.

MMS transcribed the copy she was sent and returned it to Gurney for correction, which he provided and dated it "Buire-au-Bois" (GA 64.11.71–2). Line 6 is completely changed from "One takes the air in peace, one wanders slow"; the correction agreed in letter of August/September 1917 (GA 41.126). MMS incorporated the changes in a fair copy (GA 64.11.69–70). All of the copies have "there" for "their" in 1.9. Located at Arras by WEIG.

GIRL'S SONG, p. 64
A pencil draft is in the Green Notebook (GA 64.6). Ms in letter of [?] September 1918 to MMS (*WL* 259) dated "September St Albans". The poem called "Girls Song" in the same letter was published as "The Tryst". In a letter later in September, he makes the correction of l.8. Located at Hertford by WEIG.

SOLACE OF MEN, p. 64
There are rough drafts in the Green Notebook (GA 64.6) and in the small Black Notebook (GA 64.5.6) and a Ms in a letter of [?]September 1918 to MMS (*WL* 258–9). Gurney offers an alternative last line "As poppy and mandragora it is", with its reminiscence of *Othello*, and asks "Which do you prefer?" Located in Edinburgh by WEIG.

DAY-BOYS AND CHORISTERS, p. 65
There is an early draft with Gurney's corrections of the last lines (GA 64.12.38–9), and a Ms fair copy (GA 52.11.124–124A). The years 1900–1905 were the period of Gurney's attendance at the school. He always prided himself on his prowess as a sportsman; when MMS asked him for details of his life, he listed "Centre forward for King's School", and "2nd best batting average, 3rd best bowling—last term of school" (*WL* 227).

AT RESERVE DEPOT, p. 66
Ms in letter of 12 March 1918 to MMS (GA 70.20). In l.3 the original order was "The carelessly amused passers by will see"; in a letter of 2 March 1918 to MMS he says the original line "doesn't annoy me" but

offers an alternative (GA 70.7); Ms dated "February Seaton Delaval". Located in Northumberland by WEIG.

TOASTS AND MEMORIES, p. 66

There is a draft in GA 52.1, which characteristically reads "county" for "country" in l.8. Gurney sent a transcription on 3 January 1918 to MMS (GA 41.161) dated "Seaton Delaval Nov 1917". A transcript by MMS corrects the spelling of Laventie and has Gurney's correction of l.21 (GA 64.11.80–81) and a fair copy by MMS incorporates all the changes (GA 64.11.82–3). Located in Hertford by WEIG.

FROM THE WINDOW, p. 67

There is a pencil draft of this poem in the small Black Notebook (GA 64.5.6) but I have found no fair copies. Located in Hertford by WEIG.

YPRES-MINSTERWORTH, p. 68

A pencil draft (GA 64.5.7) has been transcribed by Gurney into a fair copy (GA 64.9.2–3). There is also a typed version titled "Robecq-Minsterworth" which changes line 19 to "O wind of Somme and Lys, and Severn" (GA 64.11.10–11). Minsterworth was where the Harveys lived and the dedicateee of course F. W. Harvey. Located at Hertford by WEIG.

NEAR MIDSUMMER, p. 69

There is a pencil draft of this poem (GA 64.5.7) and Gurney's fair copy dated "Warrington July 1918" (64.9.8–9). Located at Hertford by WEIG.

TOUSSAINTS, p. 70

There is a pencil draft of stanza 1 of this poem (GA 44.3) and Gurney's fair copy dated "St Albans September 1918" (GA 64.9.18). MMS transcribed the poem in its final form (GA 64.11.147). Gurney was "anxious to know your opinion" of this poem in a letter of September 1918 (GA 61.1). Toussaints is All Saints' Day, 1 November. Located in Hertford by WEIG.

THE STONE-BREAKER, p. 71

There is a five-stanza version of this poem dated "Warrington July" (GA 64.9.1). Its first stanza reads:

> The early dew was lying yet
> Upon the grass and blossoms fair
> And fresh before the full day-heat
> The touch and fragrance of the air.

It continues with stanzas 3, 4, and 5 of the printed version and ends:

When an old man looked up, his eyes
Shining with kindness and his tone—
Mellow, West-Country, rough-edged, sweet,
England and Shakespeare's very own.

Gurney revised the poem and sent MMS an Exercise Book (the "Cannon") with two new opening stanzas and two new closing stanzas, merely noting the first word or two of stanzas 3, 4, and 5. He asks her opinion in a letter of September 1918 to MMS (GA 61.1). WEIG locates this "Ypres Hertford". The dedicatee is his younger sister.

DRIFTING LEAVES, p. 73
There is a pencil autograph copy of this dated "Warrington July 1918 (GA 64.9.13–14). Located in Gloucester by WEIG.

CONTRASTS, p. 73
There is a rough draft in the Red Notebook (GA 52.7) of which Gurney must have sent MMS a fair copy. She transcribed this and sent it back to Gurney, who made some slight alterations and added the dateline "Near Monchy" (GA 64.11.43–4). From this she has made a fair copy, taking in alterations (GA 64.11.45–46) and there is a typed copy of the same state (GA 64.11.4–5). In the "Cannon" Exercise Book, Gurney suggested a change of lines 33–4 to: "By courage keeping courage and / Hope cherishing alway" (GA 52.5) but MMS persuaded him to keep the original wording (GA 64.11.95) and copied out a final version (GA 64.11.143); on this copy the poem is dedicated "To L.D. (Good Corporal. Good Friend)". Located in Arras by WEIG.

TO F.W.H., p. 75
There is a rough pencil draft (GA 64.6) and a Ms in a letter of [?]September 1918 to MMS (*WL* 259). Gurney is obviously referring to Harvey's *A Gloucestershire Lad*. Located "Amiecourt or Hertford" by WEIG.

THE IMMORTAL HOUR, p. 75
Ms in letter of 31 July 1917 to MMS (*WL* 180–1). MMS transcribed this version and Gurney made corrections, adding "Buire-au-Bois" to her date of "July 1917" (GA 64.11.47). MMS incorporated the revisions in a fair copy (GA 64.11.48). In the "Cannon" Exercise Book (GA 52.5) Gurney sent final versions of the first two stanzas and the last two lines. The last line proved difficult; "And Joy's great fire shall" was abandoned in favour of "And feel Joy's flame cleanse the last stain of War" which was itself given up in favour of "When Joy's great flame shall cleanse the stain of war." All versions fail to escape the rhetorical. Perhaps because of the

138

rhetoric, it was published in *The Westminster Gazette* in June 1918, for which Gurney received sixteen shillings (GA 70.38.1). Located at Arras by WEIG. The dedicatee is his elder sister.

TO HIS LOVE, p. 76

There is a draft at GA 55.32–3 and a Ms in a letter of 20 January 1918 to MMS (GA 41.164), both on paper marked "Navy and Army Canteen Board". Ms dated "Seaton Delaval Northumberland Jan 1917", though the year is obviously a mistake for 1918. MMS transcribed the poem (GA 64.11.40) entering the correct date and place but deleting them, presumably for publication. Gurney subtitled the draft "On a dead Soldier" though he deleted this. Although the emotional memory of the Cotswolds and the boat are typical of Gurney's memories of F. W. Harvey, Gurney knew by this time that Harvey was in fact in a German prison camp. The draft shows Gurney's speed of working and the development of this spare poem. Lines 8–9 had read:

> Knew it. And I am sick
> Still, at the [deleted]
> Sailing the blue [deleted]

Gurney tried to end line 8 with "stamping the" and then "sailing Severn" before finding the finished state. The last stanza is remarkable for its rejection of the sentimental, and this is obviously deliberate. He had deleted after the third stanza:

> Blue bells of rich, bright trumpet
> Of daffodillies, grace
> On grace from most tender musings

and had toyed with alternatives for the end of the first line here—"grace", "triumphant"—before beginning the final version; and even there he first wrote "cover him soon / Within your heart". WEIG locates this in Hertford.

MIGRANTS, p. 77

Rough drafts in small green notebook (GA 64.6) which are transcribed into a small black notebook (GA 64.5.6) and dated "August 1918". Transcribed by Gurney in a letter of 27 August 1918 to MMS (*WL* 254–5); "Which is one of my best things—to the author's mind, at any rate", Gurney adds. Located in Hertford by WEIG.

OLD MARTINMAS EVE, p. 78

There is a fair copy by MMS of this poem as printed (GA 64.11.144v). Martinmas is the 11 November. Located at Gloucester by WEIG.

AFTER MUSIC, p. 78
Ms in letter of 8 October 1917 to MMS (*WL* 219), the first poem since Gurney returned to Britain suffering from the effects of gas. The publisher insisted on changing Gurney's "she or I" to "her or me". "The last line", he writes on 16 October 1917 (*WL* 222), "is meant to be quizzical, and is true of myself. *Is* it wise of me to play music?" Located at Ypres by WEIG.

THE TARGET, p. 79
Ms in letter of 12 October 1917 to MMS (GA 41.143). In l.16 "his" has replaced "her". MMS made a fair copy, dated "Bangour. Oct. 1917" (GA 64.11.51–2). Located in Edinburgh by WEIG.

TWIGWORTH VICARAGE, p. 79
Ms in letter of 27 August 1918 to MMS (*WL* 256), dated "St Albans August 1918". Located at Hertford by WEIG. The dedicatee, Alfred Hunter Cheesman, was vicar of Twigworth and a strong early influence on Gurney.

Hospital Pictures
Three of these promised in a letter of 29 October 1917 (GA 41.150). There is probably some memory of W. E. Henley's *In Hospital* poems; on 2 October Gurney had written to Howells when he found himself in an Edinburgh hospital "I wonder which was Henley's hospital" (*WL* 214). There was to be a seventh "Hospital Picture", but its omission was suggested by the publisher; it was called "Excursion" and is published in Kavanagh, p. 55. Alongside the dedication with its address, Gurney has noted "Written there" in WEIG.

1. LADIES OF CHARITY, p. 80
There is a Ms draft in a Black Notebook (GA 52.1) where it is called "Nurses" and has minor variants. Gurney sent a Ms in an envelope dated 17 November 1917 and addressed to MMS (GA 70.21); she transcribed it (GA 64.11.86) and made a fair copy (GA 64.11.87).

2. DUST, p. 81
There is a Ms draft in a Black Notebook (GA 52.1) with minor variants. Gurney wrote it out in a letter of 12 December 1917 to MMS (GA 70.8) where it is dated "Seaton Delaval December 1917"; and MMS made a copy with the same dateline (GA 64.11.58–9).

3. "ABERDONIAN", p. 82
Ms in letter of 31 October 1917 to MMS (*WL* 229), where it is called

"Hospital Pictures. No (1) Ulysses", and dated Bangour Hospital. Oct 1917". MMS transcribed it under that title (GA 64.11.39) Gurney added in his letter that "I hope you will like this Nielson-Kelly mixture". Nielson left the hospital about 11 October and Gurney wrote that "Nielson's wrinkled wise face and deep eyes were lovely to look at and gave me strength. Men of the sea are better to live with than the sea itelf, and through his talk, though there was nothing nautical in it, ran ever the old charm of moving salt green water, and the pictures of fearless sailors taking their chance" (GA 41.143). In the Black Notebook in which many drafts of the "Hospital Pictures" were made, Gurney noted Nielson's address at 12 Rosebank Place Aberdeen. Kelly was from Glasgow.

4. COMPANION—NORTH-EAST DUGOUT, p. 82.
Drafted in the Black Notebook (GA 52.1) with minor variations, and transcribed and sent in envelope dated 17 November 1917 to MMS (GA 70.21). She made a transcription (GA 64.11.44).

5. THE MINER, p. 83
Draft version in the Black Notebook (GA 52.1) with minor variations. Gurney sent a copy on 24 November 1917 to MMS (GA 41.155), dating it "Bangour Oct 1917". He sent another Ms in envelope dated 3 January 1918 (GA 41.161). MMS transcribed the poem, changing the date to November (GA 64.11.50). The miner was a man in whom Gurney took a keen interest, asking MMS on 26 December 1917 to send him tickets for a concert: "The chap I asked you to send a ticket to was in Hospital at Bangour with gastritis or some such thing. He was a miner, with keen interests, and a good voice, hardly any knowledge of fine music, but with fire, and a temperament that with his voice ought to go far. You would like him, I'm sure. Would you mind asking him to come and see you? He's not at all well, and most horribly depressed, what with sickness of mind and body. And a talk with sympathetic you would cheer him up no end I am sure". His name was Pte T Evans (GA 70.13).

6. UPSTAIRS PIANO, p. 83
There is an incomplete Ms draft with deletions of several lines of abandoned developments (GA 52.11.58); after l.34, for example, Gurney had written "For that a dead man sings / Of clouds and whirring wings." He copied out the poem in a letter of 3 January 1918 to MMS (GA 41.161) and dated it "Gloucester Nov 1917". MMS made a copy in which Gurney has changed "broken" to "stricken" in l.29 (GA 63.11.61–3). In WEIG Gurney notes after this poem "Best poem on Music".

HIDDEN TALES, p. 85
There are pencil drafts in both the small Black Notebook (GA 64.5.6) and

in the small Green Notebook (GA 64.6). MMS made a fair copy (GA 64.11.145). Located at Hertford by WEIG.

RECOMPENSE, p. 86
There is a pencil draft in the Black Notebook (GA 52.1) with minor variations; most corrections are made in Gurney's Ms sent on 24 November 1917 to MMS (GA 41.155). Gurney dates his transcript "Ypres-Bangour September 1917" which he then corrects by crossing out Ypres and changing the month to October. MMS made a handwritten copy (GA 64.11.42) and there is also a typed copy (GA 64.11.3). Located in Edinburgh by WEIG.

THE TRYST, p. 87
There is a pencil draft in the small Black Notebook (GA 64.5.6). Ms in letter of [?] September 1918 to MMS (*WL 258*), in a group of "new verses" dated "September St Albans", with the title "Girls Song"; stanza 3 of the printed version does not appear in this MS and the last line was "No more I'll tryst that wood." All the corrections except in the last stanza are made in a Ms of 10 September 1918 (GA 41.176), although in l.9 Gurney writes "charms", which seems to have been misread as "chains". MMS copied out a version in which corrections are made (GA 64.11.49). Located in Gloucester by WEIG. The dedicatee is Winifred Miles Chapman, for whom see *Stars in a Dark Night*.

THE PLAIN, p. 88
There is a pencil draft in the Black Notebook (GA 52.1); Gurney sent a Ms on 24 November 1917 to MMS (GA 41.155), dated "Ypres-Bangour September 1917". In MMS's transcript (GA 64.11.75) a red pen comment has questioned the repetition in l.5, "The flowers, the flowers", and l.7 "Who lie with innocence, asleep." so stimulating the changes. Located in Edinburgh by WEIG.

RUMOURS OF WARS, p. 88
Ms in letter of 3 August 1917 to MMS (GA 41.114) and dated July 1917. MMS transcribed this, and her copy was corrected by Gurney; in l.1 "Sussex" was "Surrey" (GA 64.11.65–6). Gurney dates this "Buysscheure" and MMS "July 1917". MMS made a fair copy incorporating those corrections (GA 64.11.67–8). Located in Hertford by WEIG. For Mrs Voynich see *War Letters*.

"ON REST", p. 89
Gurney's copy is in the Purple Exercise Book (GA 64.9.7–8 and 20v), dated "Warrington July" [1918]. Mentioned in letter of September 1918

to MMS (GA 61.1) where he though it had been improved. In a letter to Herbert Howells of 21 June 1916, Gurney wrote: "you cannot imagine to what a length of nervous tension we are driven. The Chinese knew a little of torture, and had an inspiration named 'Death by the thousand Cuts,' but amateurs they were besides the Grand High Inquisitors who run the British Army; which, while 'resting', has the natural aversion to wounds and death to a fear lest it should, by the anger of God, be left alive and physically fit to endure more of the same kind of 'rest'—how it hurts a man with a sense of word-values so to misuse words! It is almost as bad as 3rd grade neurasthenia" (*WL* 70). Located by WEIG "Gloucester / Vaux"

DICKY, p. 91
There is a pencil draft of this poem in the Red Notebook (GA 52.7). A transcript by MMS (GA 64.11.76) is given its title by Gurney and dated "Omiecourt. March 1917". There is a fair copy by MMS (GA 64.11.77) and a typed copy (GA 64.11.7). In a pencil list of poems in the Black Notebook (GA 52.1) Gurney lists "Dicky Rhodes". Richard Rhodes was "one of the finest little pocket corporals that ever breathed" (*WL* 148) in Gurney's opinion, and he reported in detail on his grave: "About a fortnight after the movement started, we heard his grave had been discovered; and after tea one evening the whole company (that was fit) went down for a service there. Quite a fine little wooden cross had been erected there: the Germans had done well: it was better than we ourselves would have given him; and on the cross was 'Hier ruht ein tapferer Englander, Richard Rhodes' and the date. Strange to find chivalry in sight of the destruction we had left behind us; but so it was. They must have loved his beauty, or he must have lived a little for such a tribute. But he *was* brave, and his air always gallant and gay for all his few inches. Always I admired him and his indestructibility of energy and wonderful eyes" (*WL* 152). The assocation with chivalry perhaps triggered the obvious recollection of Prince Hal's speech over Hotspur in *Henry IV Part 1*, act V, scene iv:

When that this body did contain a spirit,
A kingdom for it was too small a bound;
But now, two paces of the vilest earth
Is room enough.

Located in Edinburgh by WEIG

THE DAY OF VICTORY, p. 92
There is no Ms for this poem, which was published with minor variants in *The Gloucester Journal* of Saturday 11 January 1919, subtitled "November 11th 1918". J. W. Haines collected a typescript in his group

of poems contributed to periodicals (GA 66.20–1). WEIG annotates this "Gloucester. Night after 'Victory Day'" and "Needs amplifying".

PASSIONATE EARTH, p. 94
I have found no Ms for this poem. Located in Gloucester by WEIG. The dedicatee is John Haines.

THE POPLAR, p. 95
There is a pencil draft in the small Black Notebook (GA 64.5.6) and a Ms in a letter of September 1918 to MMS (Ga 41.184). Located in Hertford by WEIG. For the dedicatee, Marjorie ("Micky") Chapman, see *Stars in a Dark Night*.

DOWN COMMERCIAL ROAD (GLOUCESTER), p. 96
There is a pencil draft in the small Black Notebook (GA 64.5.7), from which Gurney made a pencil fair copy dated "Warrington July 1918" (GA 64.9.11–12). MMS made a fair copy (GA 64.11.146). Located in Gloucester by WEIG.

FROM OMIECOURT, p. 97
There is a pencil fair copy by Gurney in the Purple Exercise Book (GA 64.9.109), dated "July Napsbury". Located in Omiecourt in WEIG.

LE COQ FRANCAIS, p. 97
There is a pencil fair copy by Gurney in the Purple Exercise Book (GA 64.9.16–17), dated "St Albans August 1918". Located "Gloucester (or Ruy Bailleul)" in WEIG. The dedicatee is his brother.

THE FISHERMAN OF NEWNHAM, p. 98
There is a pencil draft of two stanzas in the small Black Notebook (GA 64.5.7), and a pencil fair copy by Gurney in the Purple Exercise Book (GA 64.9.6). Ms in letter of 12 July 1918 to Herbert Howells (GA 3.19). Located in Gloucester in WEIG.

THE LOCK-KEEPER, p. 99
There is a fair copy by Gurney in the Purple Exercise Book (GA 64.9.15v), dated "St Albans July 1918"; and a typed copy (GA 60.11). Located in Gloucester by WEIG.

THE REVELLERS, p. 100
I have found no Ms of this poem. Located in Gloucester by WEIG.

"ANNIE LAURIE", p. 100

Ms in letter of 12 October 1917 to MMS (GA 41.143), with minor variations. MMS made a copy of this (GA 64.11.74), dated by MMS "In Hospital. Oct 1917 Bangour"; on this Gurney made some corrections, and noted other corrections in a letter of 16 October 1917 (GA 41,147). Located in Edinburgh by WEIG. The dedicatee is Herbert Howells.

THE BATTALION IS NOW ON REST, p. 101

There is a pencil draft in the Black Notebook (GA 52.1) and a Ms in a letter of 3 January 1918 to MMS (GA 41.161). Ms dated "Seaton Delaval Nov 1917". Located in Hertford by WEIG. The dedicatee is Mrs Matilda Chapman, "La Comtesse Tilda", for whome see *Stars in a Dark Night*.

PHOTOGRAPHS, p. 102

There is a pencil draft in the Black Notebook (GA 52.1), and a Ms in a letter of 20 January 1918 to MMS (GA 41.164). "Writing it out has made me glad I did not scrap 'Photographs'", he writes; Ms dated "Seaton Delaval Dec: 1917". There is a MMS transcript for the printer (GA 64.11.60). Located in Arras by WEIG.

THAT COUNTY, p. 103

There is a pencil draft in the small Green Notebook (GA 64.6). Ms in letter to MMS dated by an editor "? Warrington July 1918" (GA 41.171) but it may well be earlier in the year. Located in Gloucester by WEIG.

INTERVAL, p. 103

There are pencil drafts of this poem in the small Black Notebook (GA 64.5.6) and in the small Green Notebook (GA 64.6). Gurney sent a Ms in a letter of 27 August 1918 to MMS (*WL* 256), dating the poem "St Albans August 1918". MMS copied the poem (GA 64.11.79), and made another transcript which makes the correction in the first line from "look up" to "how good" (GA 64.11.78). Located at Arras by WEIG.

DE PROFUNDIS, p. 104

There is a pencil draft in the small Black Notebook (GA 64.5.6) and a Ms in a letter of 10 September 1918 to MMS (GA 41.176) with the dateline "St Albans August 1918". Located at Arras by WEIG.

THE TOWER, p. 105

Gurney copied this out in his Purple Exercise Book (GA 64.9.14–15) and dated it "St Albans July 1918". Located in Gloucester by WEIG. The dedicatee is Margaret Hunt, to whom the first book was dedicated (see *The Ordeal of Ivor Gurney*).

FURTHER READING

The Story of the 2nd/5th Gloucestershire Regiment edited by A. F. Barnes, M. C., Crypt House Press, Gloucester, 1930.

Poems by Ivor Gurney with a memoir by Edmund Blunden, Hutchinson, London, 1954.

Poems of Ivor Gurney 1890-1937 with introduction by Edmund Blunden and biographical note by Leonard Clark, Chatto and Windus, London, 1973.

The Ordeal of Ivor Gurney by Michael Hurd, O. U. P., Oxford, 1978.

Collected Poems of Ivor Gurney chosen, edited and introduced by P. J. Kavanagh, O. U. P., Oxford, 1982.

Ivor Gurney War Letters edited by R. K. R. Thornton, MidNAG and Carcanet New Press, Ashington and Manchester, 1983.

"Gurney's Hobby" by Geoffrey Hill, in *Essays in Criticism*, XXXIV, No 2, April 1984.

Stars in a Dark Night: *The Letters of Ivor Gurney to the Chapman Family* edited by Anthony Boden, Alan Sutton, Gloucester, 1986.

INDEX OF TITLES
AND FIRST LINES